THE REFRACTIVE THINKER®

*Effective Business Practices for
Motivation and Communication*

THE REFRACTIVE THINKER®

VOL. VIII

Effective Business Practices for Motivation and Communication

Foreword by Ron Klein

The Refractive Thinker®: Vol. VIII: Effective Business Practices for Motivation and Communication

http://www.youtube.com/user/RefractiveThinker
https://twitter.com/refractivethnkr
https://www.facebook.com/refractivethinker

The Refractive Thinker® Press
7124 Glyndon Trail NW
Albuquerque, NM 87114 USA

info@refractivethinker.com
http://www.refractivethinker.com

CONTENTS

FOREWORD

By Ron Klein

The Academic Entrepreneur™, Dr. Cheryl Lentz, has created the next in a series of books focused on bringing research from doctoral dissertations from the coffee table to the corporate boardroom. I commend her for her dedication to doing so and this volume provides insight into the nuggets that can be gleaned from doctoral research. Let me share my perspective and thoughts.

Academia and the business world are entwined. Yet, we continue to witness a pronounced disconnect. The landscape of the workplace in the world of business and academia has historically relied on a strong work ethic. As you read each chapter herein, problems and challenges are uncovered in every sector of the work world. You will read about academia, corporate America, the health care industry, and the U.S. federal government.

The one commonality to all the challenges presented are people. They are the common thread that binds the tapestry together. They all face their own individual challenges, each with their own mindset, values, expectations, disappointments, needs, goals, and set of ethics.

Perhaps one needs to start with a basic look at communication and motivation. A significant problem is often the relationship between leaders and their followers (employees). The same holds true for professors and students. The key to successful connection is understanding and communicating effectively. The importance of listening to what people have to say is paramount to maintaining a healthy and happy work environment. Understanding each other's needs and goals makes a huge difference in relationships. What one does not understand, one cannot correct!

When you know more about the people with whom you interact, you have greater understanding, appreciation, and respect for their opinions. It's a win win situation. Appreciation is a wonderful way to move people forward. First, you give, then you get in return. Non-Profits are the perfect example. Employees have a realistic expectation that their wages will not be concomitant to For Profit wages.

Therefore, they want to be praised for working for a cause about which they are passionate and for which they make a difference. People need to know that what they do matters.

A simple formula for increased performance is:

Understanding + Communications + Motivation

=

A higher retention of high level performers

Less stress and a harmonious atmosphere result in a healthier work environment. Increased productivity and profitability are the gift behind the challenge.

Ron Klein The Grandfather of Possibilities™
and inventor of the magnetic strip on the credit card.

PREFACE

Welcome to the award winning Refractive Thinker° Doctoral Anthology Series. We are thrilled to have you join us for the 10th volume, the spring 2014 edition, as we continue to celebrate the accomplishments of doctoral scholars from around the globe.

Our mission continues to be to get research off the coffee table and into the hands of people who cannot only use, but also benefit from the many insights and wisdom found from research results. The goal is to continue to bridge the gap from the halls of academia into the halls of the business world. The Refractive Thinker° series continues to offer a resource of many doctoral scholars as they offer chapter summaries of their doctoral research well beyond the boundaries of a traditional textbook. Instead, the goal for this series is to push the boundaries beyond conventional wisdom, to explore the paths not yet traveled.

This peer-reviewed publication offers readers insights and solutions to various challenges regarding effective communication and motivation, such as how can one inspire yet maintain outcomes and results demanded by corporate executives? We hope you will find answers regarding effective strategies to help guide your efforts in the boardroom, as well as in the classroom, that have come from the research and pens of professional academicians and scholars around the world. The premise is to think not only *outside the box*, but also *beyond the box*, to create new solutions, new questions, new roads not yet explored or questioned. The topics for this volume include strategies for successful communication, job satisfaction, motivation for environmental sustainability, navigating the social exchange perspective, addressing job related stress, reasons for leadership failure, blurring the lines between business and academia, adapting to change regarding the new TQM, and discussion regarding what motivates employees to resign. Our premise is to review academic research to offer new ways for business to think about effective practices for motivation and communication.

With this volume, we add a new dimension to the series where Dr. Cheryl Lentz, *The Academic Entrepreneur*™ will introduce each chapter from an academic point of view, and Ron Klein, famous inventor and problem solver, will link this doctoral research to business application.

Remember, not only does *The Refractive Thinker* series offer a physical book, we offer eBooks (Kindle, Nook, and Adobe eReader), and eChapters that highlight the writings of your favorite Refractive Thinker® authors, available through our website: www. RefractiveThinker.com, as well as Amazon.com. Be sure to also visit our Facebook page, Twitter, our YouTube Channel, and our groups on LinkedIN for further discussions regarding the many ideas presented here.

We look forward to your continued support and interest of the more than 90 scholars within this doctoral community who contributed to the multi award winning series of *The Refractive Thinker* that began with Volume 1 so many years ago. We look forward to your stories.

ACKNOWLEDGEMENTS

The foundation of scholarly research embraces the art of asking questions---to validate and affirm, what we do, and why. Through asking the right questions, the right answers are found. Leaders often challenge the status quo, to offer alternatives and new directions, to dare to try something bold and audacious, to try something that has never been tried before. This 10th publication of our beloved award winning *Refractive Thinker®* series required the continued belief in this new publishing model, of a peer-reviewed doctoral anthology, by those willing to continue forward on this voyage.

As a result, let me express my gratitude for the help of many who made this collaboration possible.

First, let me offer a special thank you to our Peer Review Board, to include Dr. Patricia D'Urso, Dr. Judy Fisher-Blando, and Dr. Tom Woodruff, and our Board of Directors to include: Dr. Judy Fisher-Blando, Dr, Tom Woodruff, and myself. My gratitude extends to our Scholarship Committee (Dr. Susan Schild, Dr. Brian Davis, Dr. Susan Fan, and Dr. Gillian Silver) as we debut our first Refractive Thinker® Scholarship to a well deserving doctoral student to invest in the future of our doctoral community. In addition, let me offer a well-deserved thank you to our production team: Sheila Stewart International and her team, Joey Root, designer of the Refractive Thinker° logo, and our companion website designer consulting team of Tom Antion and Associates.

Dr. Cheryl Lentz

CHAPTER 1

Communicate Successfully to Motivate Effectively

By Dr. Patricia A. D'Urso and Dr. Audrey Ellison

Ralph Waldo Emerson (1944) wrote: "Trust men and they will be true to you; treat them greatly, and they will show themselves great" (p. 124). Treating employees with respect and trusting in their ability to do a *good* job, with the goal of producing high-quality products and services, will affect an organization's performance, generally leading to satisfactory outcomes, especially if a common good exists at the core of the organization. Organizational performance is a conglomeration of activities tied to a multidimensional vision, mission, and values shared by the workforce. Communicators and motivators possess many different attributes and use many different tools. These activities include employee behaviors, applied attitudes and beliefs, applied talents and skills, and patterns of communication that manifest in shared results. How people work, what people think, and what motivates people to do their work is mysterious sometimes and includes or affects the brain state of the individual at any moment in time. According to Goleman (2013), "We are constantly impacting the brain states in other people" (para. 1). To explain the Emotional Intelligence (EI) model, Goleman referred to managing relationships, implying that we are responsible for how we shape the feelings of those with whom we interact. In small groups, whether personal social groups or membership in large organizational groups, people pay attention to the person with the power and are mostly influenced by that *expressive* person. Power, charisma, rapport, positive feelings, good decision-making, and genuine caring for others are among the many necessary traits to communicate successfully with others. When communication is successful, we enhance the opportunities to change the brain states of those with whom we interact. Further, if we communicate successfully, we enhance opportunities to motivate others through the brain state change to reach higher levels of performance or goal achievement. According to Maccoby (2010), "for many, the relationship with the boss is paramount, determining the productivity of other relationships" (para. 7).

In this chapter, the authors will present findings from studies in the literature about communication and motivation as common constructs. Exploration of these two main constructs, through a pragmatic approach to analyzing these topics, was used to explore the interconnections between these two main constructs--communication and motivation--with emotional intelligence and gender as additional moderating factors and the impact all of these constructs have on employee engagement.

Overview of the Study

The purpose of this chapter is to present concomitant findings in the literature about the effects that successful communication can have on motivating employees effectively so that they can reach higher levels of performance. A model is presented that includes two major constructs and theoretical findings regarding communication and motivation, demonstrating some of the variance shared, or the interdependency and covariance of the effects of successful communication and effective motivation.

Acknowledging these widely relevant connections made about communication and motivation in the literature, and emphasizing any connection could influence the relationship of these constructs, several questions came to mind that were found appropriate to attempt to answer. What common elements do communication and motivation share at the point where communication is deemed successful and motivation is deemed effective, how does the intersect of communication and motivation affect employee engagement and performance, and does gender and/or brain activity act as moderating variables when these constructs are practiced?

Based on an extensive study by Harter, Schmidt, and Hayes (2002), there is a long-standing belief based on the evidence of their meta-analysis study, that "employee satisfaction and engagement are related to meaningful business outcomes at a magnitude that is important to many organizations" (p. 271). Harter et al. collected data from 198,514 independent employees to arrive at the findings, which included a significant correlation between employee satisfaction and engagement and overall business-unit outcomes. These authors suggested that future research should continue to include causality and directionality issues.

Communication and Motivation

A long-standing phenomenon is for-profit organizations to reward stakeholders' loyalty and strive to further the organization's good financial health and philosophical values through corporate decisions that benefit stakeholders. To accomplish this good will, management must find ways to create positive impact on performance and satisfaction (Yu, 2007). In the absence of successful communication, trust, loyalty, satisfaction and productivity, and morale can be affected. Kaplan (2007) found when management is not communicating frequently or clearly to meet employee needs for information and guidance, productivity will most likely go down. Payne (2005) suggested an increasing disconnect between workers and managers when ineffective communication exists, thus impacting employee performance. Wagner and Harter (2006) substantiated that effective communication can increase productivity 5-10%. Successful communication in and of itself is not sufficient to drive up productivity; successful communication can have an effect to motivate employees to want to perform at higher levels. Sias (2005) supported that quality and frequency of communication is related directly to motivation, and Gupta and Sharma (2008) provided similar evidence that employees who had effective interactions with leaders were more highly motivated and committed to the organization. Dasborough (2003) continued this theme with findings that open communication is critical to motivation and productivity, which leads to organizational success. Organizational success is one social reality of the way information is transformed and communicated. Significant to creating the social reality is the approach used to communicate information to the community and the follow through from manager to subordinate, setting clear expectations and building positive relationships through two-way communication to motivate. Pink (2009), during extensive research on motivation, found that employees are motivated by the intrinsic rewards of mastering a task. In earlier work, Maccoby (1988, 1995) suggested that to motivate followers, "leaders should employ a mix of four Rs: Responsibilities, Relationships, Rewards, Reasons" (Abstract). Intrinsic and extrinsic aspects of motivation will have varying degrees of success when applied. For example, acknowledging the work of Harlow (1949) with rhesus monkeys at the University of Wisconsin, and Deci's (1975), work with students at Carnegie-Mellon, Pink (2009) found that extrinsic rewards--bananas or money-depress problem-solving performance, respectively, were not as effective as the intrinsic rewards of mastering a task, which was more engaging. Pink acknowledged that this thesis fits in some contexts but not others.

Motivation, Communication, and Engaged Employees

In the 21st century workplace, it has become critical for organizations to manage human assets. Motivating knowledge workers requires communication between employees and managers. However, motivation is not easy. Retaining skilled workers can be costly (Jacobson, 2011). Grigoryev (2006) reported that 46% of new hires failed within the first 18 months based on low levels of emotional intelligence (23%) and other demotivational issues rather than lack of competence (11%). Retaining the appropriate employees is connected to motivating employees. Employee retention is not a *soft* skill, it is a bottom-line issue for companies. Lack of employee commitment and disengagement can be costly. People do not leave companies, they leave managers (Smith, 2006). Effective leadership is a factor in employee retention and emotional intelligence is a factor in effective leadership (Sengupta, 2011). Therefore, emotional intelligence can affect organizational commitment and employee engagement. Emotionally intelligent leaders motivate employee growth and development. The leader's emotional intelligence has a direct influence on employee motivation and organizational commitment (Ruiz-Palomino & Martinez, 2011).

Effective leaders and managers inspire and motivate employees to achieve personal and organizational goals. EI is correlated to organizational commitment and employee engagement (Sarkar, 2011), as it plays a role in influencing employees to achieve higher goals. EI leaders can help employees reach their full potential thus affecting job satisfaction and motivation. Cherniss and Goleman

(2001) found that "EI accounts for 85-90 percent of the success of organizational leaders" (p. xv). Oreg and Berson (2011) found that the leader's level of EI has a 12% positive impact on employee motivation. Therefore, training leaders in EI can help in motivating employees to strive for excellence (Lacity, Iyer, & Rudramuniyaiah, 2008). Emotionally intelligent managers and employees communicate effectively with others, breaking down personal and organizational barriers of unknoEffective communication and interaction have a positive effect on employee performance and job satisfaction (Yu, 2007); effective communication, especially, can drive productivity. Ineffective communication negatively impacts performance and satisfaction. Employees are more highly motivated and committed to the organization when they have effective interactions with leaders (Gupta & Sharma, 2008). Manager and employee communication is the foundation for increasing organizational effectiveness; failure to communicate or to communicate negatively impacts employee performance. Managers need to communicate effectively and frequently to raise levels of performance and productivity (Davis & Rothstein, 2006).

However, in today's workplace electronic communication is increasing while face-to-face communication is decreasing. Yet, Therkelsen and Friebich (2003) found that face-to-face communication is most effective for increasing satisfaction and productivity. With electronic communication, we focus on the message while losing the feelings and attitudes behind the words. There is a link between emotional intelligence and effective communication. EI is related to communication and gender (Rothbard & Wilk, 2011). In their meta-analysis study, Joseph and Newman (2010) reminded the reader that skepticism sometimes surrounds the theoretical bases of this construct, Emotional Intelligence. Tantamount to answering the research questions posed in this study, that of a connection of communication, motivation, EI by gender, and a connection of these constructs to employee engagement, we learned that Joseph and Newman examined gender and race-based subgroup differences in EI. These authors also addressed the issues of whether or not EI tests can favor women and if EI is a better predictor of job performance in high emotional jobs. Their findings were not theoretically strong and therefore inconclusive that EI could be used as a predictor of job performance. The findings support the common assumption that EI scores tend to be higher among women than men; however, "a substantial amount of evidence exists regarding sex differences on overall EI, very little empirical work has been reported on sex differences in EI dimensions" (p. 45). Joseph and Newman also suggested additional research to examine relationships between other constructs such as self-efficacy and achievement motivation and EI.

A non-profit organization, SixSeconds (2012), focused on practicing emotional intelligence, found that women have advantages in some areas of emotional intelligence, while men have advantages in other areas. Women have a slight edge to assess emotional data, selecting an emotional response and applying emotional significance. Men do better harnessing the insights and moving forward with intention. Women have an important opportunity for creating added value and building workplaces where people thrive. Rosener (2011) offered the results of a recent survey, sponsored by the International Women's Forum (IWF) on leadership that uncovered a number of unexpected similarities exist between men and women leaders along with important differences, not the least of which is leadership style and how the women influence those with whom they work. One specific sense of how to motivate employees was reported in this IWF survey that women "described themselves in ways that characterize 'transformational' leadership, influencing subordinates to transform their own self-interest into the interest of the group" (p. 20). Enthusiasm for the interest of the group must be stimulated; in other words, leaders and managers must move from talk to action and motivate employees to engage in the interest of the whole organization and its strategically-planned outcomes.

Disengaged employees can cause havoc and tamper with morale. "Gallup estimates that these actively disengaged employees cost the U.S. between $450 billion to $550 billion each year in lost productivity. They are more likely to steal from their companies, negatively influence their coworkers, miss workdays, and drive customers away" (Lipman, 2013, para. 2). The Gallup, Inc. researchers also found that 70% of workers are disengaged. Emotional intelligence is one of the drivers of employee engagement, and emotional intelligent leaders manage relationships and communication more effectively. The EI leaders motivate employees to strive for high goals. They develop employees that are committed to the organization and satisfied with their jobs. The work of engaged employees directly effects the bottom-line with reduced turnover and increased retention.

Communication, Motivation, and Brain Connections by Gender

Communication is at the center of social life: accomplishment, challenges, and changes in social life. Communication is one of the most powerful agents for change and can help to address the inequities and problems in our social life and bring pleasure and joy to an otherwise mundane day. According to Wood (2010), "Critical research has given us insight into ways in which communication practices sustain male dominance in conversations and ways that organizational structures and practices create hostile work environments for women and minorities" (p. 15).

The objective is not to emphasize the inequities in life; the point is to convince the reader about the power of communication. Male and female communication patterns are evident in professional and personal interactions with contingent influence from external variables such as race, religion, culture, heredity, economic class, education, and sexual orientation. In the search for best communication practices in the workplace, it is important to understand similarities and dissimilarities exist among male and female communication patterns for a number of reasons, not the least of which is how the male and female brains are wired to communicate. According to Gong, He, and Evans (2011), "male and female brains display differences in the network topology that represent the organizational patterns of brain connectivity across the entire brain" (Abstract), which could explain gender-related cognitive differences. According to Herrmann (1996), researchers are fascinated with communication, gender, and brain wiring relative to communication and continue to add to the literature on this subject; many such studies introduce psychometric instruments as a tool to provide scientific evidence to prove and satisfy such hypotheses. To offer one example, the Herrmann Brain Dominance Instrument (HBDI) is a neuropsychological assessment that measures thinking styles relative to the whole brain; this instrument is used to evaluate and diagnose neuropsychological and cognitive processes of thinking and these thinking styles can translate and transform into communication patterns. Understanding the principle of these mental processes "presents a unique new method of diagnosing business situations and provides an understanding of key business and leadership issues that have resisted meaningful measurement until now" (Herrmann, 1996, p. 3). Two significant measurements are: the differences between male and female communication patterns and, if and to what extent, do these differences affect business outcomes.

One key business and leadership issue is communication and how males and females are *wired* to communicate. Hotz (2013) contended "no one knows how gender variations in brain wiring translate into thought and behavior" (p. 1), but acknowledged the significant controversy that surrounds the topic. Evidence is mounting about this topic of gender differences in brain wiring; Jahanshad et al. (2011) in their work with neuroimaging, provided convincing evidence that neural connections differ by gender. At the proceedings of the National Academy of Sciences at the University of Pennsylvania, Thompson (2011), part of the Jahanshad research group, explained the variations in how men and women respond to various issues in life; these responses can be extrapolated to how men and women communicate, verbalizing those responses or reactions. To substantiate this theory, the research conducted at the University of Pennsylvania has shown different patterns of brain connections among young men and young women but not much difference in childhood; rather, most of the male-female brain differences occur in adolescence. "The observations suggest that male brains are structured to facilitate connectivity between perception and coordinated action, whereas female brains are designed to facilitate communication between analytical and intuitive processing modes" (Ingalhalikar, et al., 2013, Abstract). Many study teams continue to research male and female brain wiring and how brain wiring affects communication and motivation behaviors.

The realization that the female brain is wired to facilitate communication between analytical and intuitive processing modes can provide appreciation and instrumentality for how females communicate and therefore how they motivate. The utility of interaction is an important consideration because communication influences and motivates employees to perform at standard and above-standard levels and therefore, ultimately, effects organizational outcomes and competitive advantage. How employees are motivated, through the use of effective communication patterns, can be a predictor of job performance and satisfaction, and specifically can be used as a prescription for how organizations communicate and motivate by gender. The more opportunities an organization has to cultivate collaboration between genders, the greater the probability that there will be a strong individual propensity to invest energy in that collaborative work, which can lead to significant business outcomes. LeBouc and Pessiglione (2013) offered this hypothesis in their work with imaging social motivation and distinct brain mechanisms of drive effort. LeBouc and Pessiglione suggested that cognitive mechanisms that motivate effort production remain poorly understood; they emphasized the notion that motivation can be reduced to experience personal utility of effort production; this was a significant finding in their work because of magnetic resonance imaging of the brain. Further substantiation of the connection between brain wiring and motivation was introduced by LeDoux (2012) in his continuing work on brain wiring and his belief that motivation is an assessed behavior and "involves approach toward desired outcomes and avoidance of undesired outcomes" (p. 660). Organizations are not gender neutral; differences in behaviors by gender exist, and organizations could benefit by capitalizing on strengths that are manifest by variant differences (LeBouc & Pessiglione, 2013; Rennison, 2014). These differences are one important focus of this chapter.

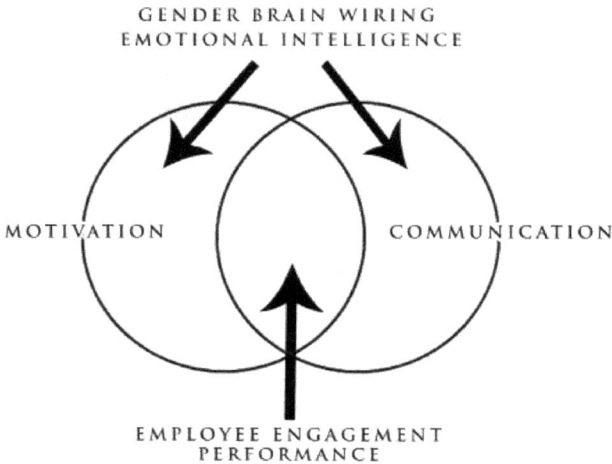

Figure 1: Shared Variance Model illustrates the constructs of motivation and communication and the shared variance of these two constructs that also includes degrees of influence on employee engagement and performance as moderated by gender brain wiring and emotional intelligence. Adapted by P. D'Urso and A. Ellison, 2014.

There are numerous common elements that surfaced in this capture, which suggested employee engagement and high performance intersect with motivation and communication. Likewise, there were numerous possibilities for the variables to share common elements that contribute to motivation. The model demonstrates the variables of gender and brain wiring and emotional intelligence, as is the focus of the literature review.

Synthesis. Analyses of many different studies in the literature on brain wiring, and how the wiring affects communication and motivation patterns in males and females, continued to point to the fact that brain activity by gender should not be dismissed without consideration. The difference in brain wiring by gender is a partial and viable explanation for how people communicate and motivate. The understanding of behavior in the workplace is complex and requires an awareness that many different factors provoke and influence how employees work, many of which have been discussed in this chapter. Intriguing is the fact that there is significant interconnectedness in the literature about communication and motivation that incidentally continues to show up. We have not found anything striking, remarkable or new in the review; rather we have attempted to be precise and accurate about sharing observations about this interconnectedness between and among communication, motivation, emotional intelligence, brain wiring by gender, and finally the affects these factors have on employee engagement and performance!

Thoughts from the Academic Entrepreneur ™

The problem to be solved:

- Ineffective communication and motivation strategies

The goals:

- Learning effective communication strategies to motivate employees to achieve higher levels of performance in business.

The questions to ask:

- How can organizations affect employee engagement and performance?
- Does gender and/or brain activity act as moderating variables when these constructs are practiced?

Today's Business Application:

- Trust your employees to do a good job, and show them that they have your trust.

- Model the traits that you want your team to have within your own behavior.
- Cultivate channels for employee feedback, and act visibly on that feedback.

References

Cherniss, C., & Goleman, D. (2001). *The emotionally intelligent workplace: How to measure, and improve emotional intelligence in individuals, groups and organizations.* San Francisco, CA: Jossey–Bass.

Dasborough, M. T. (2003). Cognitive asymmetry in employee affective reactions to leadership behaviors. *The Center for Creative Leadership.* Retrieved from http://www.ccl.org/leadership

Davis, A. L., & Rothstein, H. R. (20006). The effects of perceived behavioral integrity of managers on employee attitudes: A meta-analysis. *Journal of Business Ethics, 67*, 407-419. doi:10.1007/s10551-006-9034-4

Deci, E. L. (1975). *Intrinsic motivation.* New York, NY: Plenum.

Emerson, R. W. (1944). *The essays of Ralph Waldo Emerson.* New York, NY: Random House, Inc. (cited in essays by Ralph Waldo Emerson, A Penn State Electronic Classics Series Publication). Retrieved from http://www2.hn.psu.edu/faculty/jmanis/rw-emerson/essays_rwe.pdf

Goleman, D. (2013). *The social brain. LinkedIn.* http://www.linkedin.com/today/post/article/20130201162026-117825785-the-social-brain

Gong, G., He, Y., & Evans, A .C. (2011, October). Brain connectivity: Gender makes a difference. *Neuroscientist, 17*, 575-591. doi:10.1177/1073858410386492

Grigoryev, P. (2006). Hiring by competency models. *The Journal for Quality and Participation, 29*(4), 16-18.

Gupta, B., & Sharma, N. K. (2008). Compliance with base of power and subordinates' perception of superiors: Moderating effect of quality of interaction. *Singapore Management Review, 30*(1), 1-24.

Harter, J. K., Schmidt, F. L., & Hayes, T. L. (2002). Business-unit-level relationship between employee satisfaction, employee engagement, and business outcomes: A meta-analysis. *Journal of Applied Psychology, 87*(2), 268-279. doi:10.1037/0021-9010.87.2.268

Herrmann, N. (1996). *The whole brain business book.* Boston, MA: McGraw-Hill.

Hotz, R. L. (2013, December 10). Brain wiring in men versus women. *Wall Street Journal.* Retrieved from http://online.wsj.com/news/articles/SB100 01424052702304744304579248151866594232

Ingalhalikar, M., Smith, A., Parker, D., Satterthwaite, T. D., Elliott, M. A., Ruparel, K., . . . Verma, R. (2013). Sex differences in the structural connectome of the human brain. *PNAS 2013; published ahead of print December 2, 2013,* Biological Sciences-Neuroscience :Madhura Ingalhalikar, doi:10.1073/pnas.1316909110

Jacobson, W. S. (2011). Creating a motivated workforce: How organizations could enhance and develop public service motivation. *Public Personnel Management, 40*(3), 215-238

Jahanshad, N., Aganj, I., Lenglet, C., Joshi, A., Yan Jin, Barysheva, M., ... Thompson, P.M. (2011, March 30). Sex differences in the human connectome: 4-Tesla high angular resolution diffusion imaging (HARDI) tractography in 234 young adult twins. *Biomedical Imaging: From Nano to Macro, 2011 IEEE International Symposium,* 939-943. doi:10.1109/ISBI.2011.5872558

Joseph, D. L., & Newman, D. A. (2010). Emotional intelligence: An integrative meta-analysis and cascading model. *Journal of Applied Psychology, 95*(1), 54-78. doi:10.1037/a0017286

Kaplan, R. S. (2007). What to ask the person in the mirror. *Harvard Business Review, 1,* 1-9.

Lacity, M. C., Iyer, V. V., & Rudramuniyaiah, P. S. (2008). Employees' motivation of Indian IS professionals. *Information Systems Frontiers. 10*(2), 225-241. doi:10.1007/s10796-007-9062-3

LeBouc, R., & Pessiglione, M. (2013, October 2). Imaging social motivation: Distinct brain mechanisms drive effort production during collaboration versus competition. *The Journal of Neuroscience, 33,* 15894-15902. doi:10.1523/JNeurosci.0143-13.2013

LeDoux, J. (2012). Rethinking the emotional brain, *Neuron, 73,* 653-676. doi:10.1016/j.neuron.2012.02.004

Lipman, V. (2013, September/23). Surprising, disturbing facts from mother of all employee engagement surveys. Retrieved from http://www.

forbes.com/sites/victorlipman/2013/09/23/surprising-disturbing-facts-from-the-mother-of-all-employee-engagement-surveys/

Maccoby, M. (2010). 4 Rs of motivation. *Research Technology Management, 53*(4), 60-61.

Maccoby, M. (1995). *Why work?: Motivating the new workforce.* Alexandria, VA: Miles River Press.

Maccoby, M. (1988). Why work: Leading the new generation. New York, NY: Simon & Schuster.

Oreg, S., & Berson, Y. (2011). Leadership and employees' reactions to change: The role of leaders' personal attributes and transformational leadership style. *Personality Psychology, 64,* 627-659. doi:10.1111/j.1744-6570.2011.01221.x

Payne, H. J. (2005). Reconceptualizing social skills in organizations: exploring the relationship between communication competence, job performance and supervisory roles. *Journal of Leadership and Organizational Studies, 11,* 63-77. doi:10.1177/107179190501100207

Pink, D. H. (2009). *Drive: The surprising truth about what motivates us.* New York, NY: Penguin-Riverhead.

Rennison, B. W. (2014). Cracking the gender codes: Discourses of women in management. Accepted for publication in peer-reviewed journal: *Gender, Work, and Organization.*

Rosener, J. B. (2011). Ways women lead. In Werhane, P., Painter-Morland, M. (Eds.), Chapter 3 (pp. 19-29). *Leadership, Gender, and Organization, 27,* 19-29 19-29. doi:10.1007/978-90-481-9014-0_3

Rothbard, N. P., & Wilk, S. L. (2011). Waking up on the right or wrong side of the bed: Start-of-workday mood, work events, employee affect, and performance. *Academy of Management Journal, 54,* 959-980. doi:10.5465/amj.2007.0056

Ruiz-Palomino, P., & Martinez, R. (2011). Supervisor role modeling, ethics-related organizational policies, and employee ethical intention: The moderating impact of moral ideology. *Journal of Business Ethics, 102,* 653-668. doi:10.1007/s10551-011-0837-6

Sarkar, S. (2011). A study on employee engagement at manufacturing industries. *Global Management. Review, 5*(3), 62-72.

Sengupta, S. S. (2011). Growth in human motivation: Beyond Maslow. *Indian Journal Industrial Relations, 47*(1), 102-116.

Sias, P. M. (2005). Workplace relationship quality and employee information experiences. *Communication Studies, 56,* 375-395. doi:10.1080/10510970500319450

SixSeconds. (2012). Retrieved from http://www.6seconds. org/?s=women (2012)

Smith, I. (2006). Communicating in times of change. *Library Management, 27*(1/2), 108-112. doi:10.1108/01435120610647992

Therkelsen D. J., & Fiebich, C. L. (2003). The supervisor: The linchpin of employee relations. *Journal of Communication Management, 8*(2), 120-129.

Wagner, R., & Harter, J. K. (2006). *12: the elements of great managers,* Princeton, NJ: The Gallup Press.

Wood, J. T. (2010). *Gendered lives: Communication, gender and culture.* (10th ed.). Boston, MA: Cengage.

Yu, L. (2007). Intelligence: The benefits of a coaching culture. *MIT Sloan Management Review, 48*(2), 6.

About the Author...

Dr. Audrey Ellison grew up in NY, lived in CT and MA before moving to Tampa, FL. She earned her doctorate in marketing from Nova Southeastern University. She holds an MBA from Simmons College, a Masters of Library Science and BS in History from Southern Connecticut State University. She is a certified facilitator in emotional intelligence, quality management, leadership, and extraordinary customer relations. She was trained as a Baldrige examiner. She has received training in SPIN selling, Situational Leadership and Herrmann Brain Dominance. She earned certificates from Columbia University Executive Education in marketing and USC/Times Mirror Leadership Institute.

Dr. Audrey teaches marketing and management courses at the University of Phoenix. She has received Outstanding Faculty Award and honored as one of the top ten instructors (top 1%) in Florida. In the past, she managed a winning state senate candidate, worked on a successful U.S. Senate campaign, and organized an Executive Study Tour to visit Deming Prize winning companies in Japan.

Dr. Audrey is a marketing strategist and consultant working with organizations to develop and implement marketing strategies. She coaches managers to improve their communication and management skills, and entrepreneurs in creating their business. She has conducted training sessions/webinars on communication.

To reach Dr. Audrey Ellison for information on consulting or doctoral coaching, please e-mail: ae@mosaicmktgbay.com

About About the Author...

Dr. Patricia A. D'Urso is a native of Pennsylvania and has worked in academe since 1970. Pat earned a Ph.D., in Adult Education with a cognate in research and measurement (stats) at the University of South Florida. She earned a Master's of Business Administration with a concentration in management from Penn State, A Master's of Science in Psychology from the University of Phoenix, and a Bachelor's of Science degree in Industrial and Labor Relations with an economics minor from the State University of New York at Cortland. She holds a Supervision Certification from Cornell University, a Green Belt in Six Sigma from Villanova University, and has completed the course work for the Black Belt certification through the American Society of Quality.

Dr. Pat is a linear analyst, teaches doctoral students in research and measurement, organizational behavior and development, and leadership courses at two for-profit universities. Her personal research topics include trust and respect in the workplace and communication, motivation and brain wiring. She consults with organizational clients on statistical analyses, and enjoys her work with the doctoral students she chairs and serves as committee member or as teaching faculty.

To reach Dr. Pat D'Urso for information on her research topics of interest or questions regarding the doctoral journey, please contact her at http://Dursoconsultancy.com or e-mail: pat.durso@gmail.com

CHAPTER 2

Bridging the Job Satisfaction Gap: What U.S.
Federal Leaders Need to Know

By Dr. Sheila G. Embry

Since 2010, U.S. federal employees faced budget cuts, hiring slowdowns, equipment purchase moratoriums, increased worker pension costs, a three-year pay freeze, and a 16-day unpaid furlough (Hicks, 2014; Fox, 2014). U.S. federal employee job satisfaction, which closed to within five points of U. S. private sector employee job satisfaction index points in 2010, dropped "to an all-time low, erasing the hard-won gains"(Shane, 2013, p. 1). With 30% of the U.S. federal workforce eligible for retirement in the next 3 years, U.S. federal employee job satisfaction is critical. "An uptick in retirements is being fueled by $85 billion in spending cuts, along with furloughs, pay freezes, slashed overtime, and increased work load from the lack of new hires" (Liberto, 2013, p. 2). To keep government services continuing at the expected level, an increase U.S. federal employee job satisfaction is required.

U.S. federal employee job satisfaction dropped 7.2 points in the *2013 Best Places to Work in the Federal Government* report showing losses in 10 categories including strategic management, effective leadership, skills-mission match, teamwork, and work-life balance. Two areas of concern: only 44% of U.S. federal employees responded they had sufficient resources to do their job, and less than 1/3 responded that job-relevant knowledge and skills to accomplish organizational goals were present (Shane, 2013).

As shown in Figure 1, the latest drop created a 12.9 point gap in job satisfaction between U.S. federal employees and U.S. private sector employees (Shane, 2013). Index scores were 57.8% for U.S. federal employee job satisfaction and 70.7% for U. S. private sector workers (Hicks, 2014). Despite these low percentages, 88% of U.S. federal workers continued to believe that the work they did was important (Shane, 2013).

EMPLOYEE JOB SATISFACTION 2009-2013

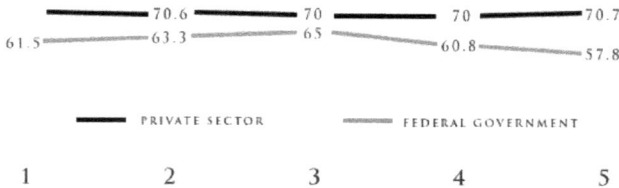

		1	2	3	4	5
INDEX SCORE		2009	2010	2011	2012	2013
PRIVATE SECTOR		71.2	70.6	70	70	70.7
FEDERAL GOVERNMENT		61.5	63.3	65	60.8	57.8

Figure 1: Comparison of job satisfaction index scores between U.S. federal and U. S. private sector employees according the 2013 Partnership of Public Service report, Best Places to Work in the Federal Government.

U.S. federal employees understand what is going on in their organizations, and the majority believes in the public servants' mission. The low job satisfaction report results were warnings from U.S. federal employees that many U.S. federal agencies are not able to meet the needs of its stakeholders and clients (Shane, 2013). "We're seeing this massive brain drain as thousands of workers leave the U.S. federal workforce, and it's leading to a huge loss of knowledge and expertise," said William Dougan, President of the National Federation of U.S. Federal Employees (Liberto, 2013, p. 2). U.S. federal supervisors should create a work environment that encourages retirement-eligible employees to share institutional knowledge with new employees before leaving the U. S. federal workforce.

Background

In 2013, 2.1 million employees worked for the U.S. federal government. Leadership; employee engagement and job satisfaction; and belief in the mission of the agency were 3 of the 10 categories studied in the *Best Places to Work in the Federal Government* report. Published by Partnership for Public Service, the *Best Places Work in the Federal Government* report was based on data collected from the Office of Personnel Management's *Federal Employee Viewpoint* survey conducted between April 2013 and June 2013.

The *Best Places to Work in the Federal Government* report ranked agencies via index scores (1 to 100) based on responses to questions in 10 areas: effective leadership, employee skills–mission match, pay, strategic management, teamwork, training and development, work-life balance, support for diversity, and performance-based rewards and advancement. U.S. federal employees consistently chose effective leadership as the most important issue, followed by employee skills matching with agency mission. From 2003 to

2010, U.S. federal employees chose work-life balance as the third most important issue for ranking. Conversely, since 2010, pay, awards, and equitable promotions were listed as the third most important issue (Partnership for Public Service, 2013).

The 2009 Embry study, presented in partial fulfillment for a doctorate of management degree, was a mixed-method study at a large U.S. federal agency that examined U.S. federal employee performance and morale. The population included U.S. federal employees, supervisors, and executives who worked within one U.S. federal agency directorate headquartered in Washington, DC. The goal was to test the correlation between the predictor variables of perceived supervisor leadership and communication and the criterion variable of employee performance (Embry, 2009).

The Supervisory Leadership Communication Inventory (SLCI), developed by Rouse and Schuttler (2009), included 53 questions that measured supervisory leadership and employee performance and 3 opened-ended questions that allowed participants to offer comments, suggestions, and recommendations for better employee performance. Over 35 days, data were collected from 435 individuals with an 87% ($n = 378$) completion rate, which exceeded the target population by 12 respondents. The SLCI's Cronbach alpha was .82, indicating the measures were sufficiently reliable for conducting the statistical analysis (Embry, 2009).

Results listed in the Partnership for Public Service report (2013) and the Embry study (2009) will be reviewed in the next section. Recommendations from the 2013 report will be compared with recommendations from the 2009 study. Additionally, 2013 recommendations for the agency that was studied in 2009 will be reviewed to determine if any change has been made in U.S. federal employee viewpoints.

Study Agency

In the 2009 Embry study of a U.S. federal agency directorate with more than 7,600 U.S. federal workers, one of the questions respondents were asked was how, if at all, can leaders improve employee performance? Respondents ranged from clerical employees (GS-5) through executives (SES) and in multiple regions of the United States: North East, South East, Central, Western, and Headquarters (Washington, DC). Respondents were 61% non-managerial and 39% management (Embry, 2009).

Qualitative responses indicated effective leadership, management visibility, and management attentiveness were top themes to improve employee performance. In an area used to collect comments and suggestions, better training and education for managers and supervisors was the number one suggestion. Other popular suggestions included creating a better hiring practice, and recognition of the communication confusion between supervisors who state quality is important but who continue to rate and discipline on production numbers. Additional comments mentioned that listening to employees would increase morale. As shown in Figure 2, the study results inferred (a) a proven correlation between supervisory communication and employee and organization performance; (b) employee morale and job satisfaction were directly tied to supervisory relationship, communication, and leadership; and (c) employee performance could be improved with increased supervisor leadership and training within both areas (Embry, 2009).

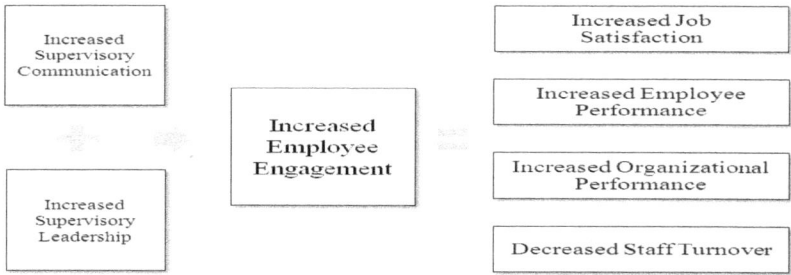

Figure 2. Correlation between supervisor leadership, communication, and employee/organizational performance. 1

Additionally, O'Connor (2006) stated to improve employee morale supervisors should communicate more about the employees' positions within the organization's mission and assist with training opportunities and other strategies to address skill deficiencies. Major (2007) determined relationships between supervisors and employees were one of the critical elements for positive employee morale and performance. Colbert (2008) found that when supervisors exhibited a positive influence by motivation, inspiration, and commitment to concern for employees' intellectual opportunities and professional needs, employees' morale increased, and employees were more engaged in the organizations' vision, mission, strategies, and goals.

Finally (Rosenberg, 2009a, 2009b) showed that highly rated employees were four times as likely to leave organizations if not engaged. Timely distribution of critical information, ongoing exchanges between employees and supervisors helped built trust and camaraderie between employees and supervisors. Timely distribution of critical information, and ongoing

1 From Embry, S. (2009). *A Mixed Method Study: Understanding Employee Performance at the Department of Homeland Security,* UMI Publications. Copyright 2009 by Dr. Sheila G. Embry. Reprinted with permission.

exchanges between employees and supervisors also helped control stressful situations and demonstrated professionalism and tact (Embry, 2009).

In line with these findings recommendations from the 2009 Embry study posited to increase employee morale and performance, supervisors must communicate to their employees that their jobs are of critical importance to the mission of the agency and to define how employees fit within agency goals. Targeted relationship building, assessments in communication and leadership, and training for all levels of leaders – supervisors, managers, and executives – should be implemented to address the gap between headquarters leadership and field employee perceptions and performance. If supervisors increased their leadership and communication knowledge and skills, employee performance increased (Embry 2009). Employees who were valued and have higher morale were more likely to engage in organizations and were more likely to give higher rating to their performance and their organization's performance (Brodsky & Newell, 2009).

Since 2010, a U.S. federal agency's leaders committed to improving relationships with the agency's employees. To solicit employee feedback and improve communication, agency leaders and supervisors held meetings, national town halls in various locations around the country, employee-leader working groups, surveys, and communities of practice. In response to these communications, agency leadership (a) revised telework and alternative work schedule programs; (b) emphasized career development via individual development plans; (c) created agency mentoring and coaching programs; (d) revised training programs for supervisors; (e) created a new employee onboarding program; (f) improved relationships with the employee unions; and (g) instructed supervisors to tie employee contributions to the agency mission during performance reviews.

During the same time, agency backlogs reduced, processes streamlined, and the agency ranking improved. In 2007, the agency ranked in the low 15%, i.e., 189 out of 222 U.S. federal agency subcomponents (Embry, 2009). In 2013, the agency moved up to 76 out of 300 U.S. federal agency subcomponents, putting it in the upper 58% of *Best Places to Work in the Federal Government.* Strengths from the 2013 survey for this agency included (a) 97% of the respondents stated, "When needed, I am willing to put in the extra effort to get a job done." (b) 93% of the respondents stated, "I am constantly looking for ways to do my job better." (c) 91% of the respondents stated, "The work I do is important." (d) 86% of the respondents stated, "I know how my work relates to the agency's goals and priorities." and (e) 85% of the respondents stated, "I am held accountable for achieved results" (Partnership for Public Service, 2013).

In the 2009 study, respondents listed the following six areas the agency needed to improve to increase employee morale: (a) effective leadership, management visibility, management attentiveness, training for supervisors; (b) hiring practices; and (c) communication, and listening to employees (Embry, 2009). Four of these areas concerned supervisors while two of the areas concerned communication with employees. In the 2013 *Best Places to Work in the Federal Government* report, respondents ranked the areas for agency improvements to increase U.S. federal employee job satisfaction: (a) pay raises (50%), (b) poor performers who will not improve (40%), (c) differences in performance recognized in a meaningful way (38%), (d) promotions based on merit, (37%), and (e) potential for getting a better job within the organization (33%) (Partnership for Public Service, 2013).

What was not listed in the top four 2013 survey results were concerns about leadership that were in the 2009 Embry study.

Concerns about the employees' financial and professional futures topped the list of challenges for the agency. The change in findings could be in response to the communication work of the agency leaders and supervisors, or in response to fiscal and political environments – three years without a pay increase, budgets and awards severely cut, hiring slowdown and equipment purchase slowdowns. "Without a more predictable and responsible budget situation, we risk our most talented employees as well as hurting our ability to recruit top talent for the future" (Hicks, 2014, p. 2). Changes in rankings cannot be validated in the current fiscal environment.

Other Agencies

U.S. federal employee job satisfaction averages for 371 agencies dropped 3 points to 57.8% on a scale of 100 government-wide in 2013, the lowest since rankings were collected in 2003. Satisfaction with pay dropped 4.7 points. The second largest area of decline involved satisfaction with training and development that fell 3.2 points in 2013. The third largest area of decline involved satisfaction in performance-based rewards and advancement that dropped 2.2 points. In 2013, strategic management dropped 2.1 points government-wide, effective leadership dropped 1.0 nationally, and training and education dropped 3.2 points. Specific rankings: (a) effective leadership dropped 1 point, (b) effective leadership–empowerment dropped 2 points, (c) effective leadership–fairness dropped .4 points, (d) effective leadership–senior leaders dropped 1.3 points, (e) effective leadership–supervisors dropped .5 points, (f)employee skills–mission match dropped 2.1 points, (g) pay dropped 4.7 points, (h) strategic management dropped 2.1 points, (i) teamwork dropped .5 points, (j) training and development dropped 3.2 points, (k) work-life balance dropped 1.8 points, (l) support for diversity dropped .7 points, (m) performance-based rewards/advancement dropped 2.1 points, and (n) alternative work/employee-support programs dropped .4 points (Partnership for Public Service, 2013).

Recommendations

U.S. federal agencies that ranked low in the *Best Places to Work in the Federal Government* report should take lessons from improving agencies. Assuming congressional budgeting, which was "much of the management dysfunction in government" (Hicks, 2014, p. 2) for the last 3 years' continues, improving U.S. federal employee job satisfaction will be largely up to agency leaders in areas other than pay raises. Leaders should look at the agency's communication plan for improvements. Are supervisors talking regularly with their employees? More importantly, are supervisors listening to employees? Other areas include adding employees into strategic planning, training and development, and innovations (Partnership for Public Service, 2013).

Increased supervisor-employee communication. When supervisors disengaged, employees did not know or were confused about what to do to complete the agency mission based on the agency vision. Information was critical to success. Listening to employees was important to supervisor-employee communication and engagement. Employees were more likely to be engaged with engaged supervisors (Schuttler, 2010). Once employees and supervisors were engaged, employee job satisfaction increased.

The U.S. Patent and Trademark Office moved from 172 out of 222 agencies in 2007 to 1 out of 300 agencies in 2013. During the same time, agency leaders increased supervisory communication, supervisory training, and included supervisors in management decisions (Partnership for Public Service, 2013). To begin supervisor-employee communication, build productive relationships with employee unions; create avenues for feedback such as meetings, town halls, employee committees, working groups, and suggestion boxes; and implement employee mentoring programs (Fox, 2014). Communication is not just the verbal or written message. The way the message is delivered is part of communication. Was the message credible? Was the message consistent? Was the message delivered with courtesy? Supervisors must consider the effect of the message as well as the words of the message (Embry, 2009).

Supervisors must be trusted by employees. Without trust, the message will not be heard. Treat and communicate with employees professionally, with dignity, and with respect. Employees' morale and job satisfaction will improve (Schuttler, 2010). The U.S. Trade and Development Agency is a small agency with 50 employees and an example of one agency that allowed employees to assist with strategic planning. Annual strategic planning sessions were attended by employees who determined the priorities for the following year (Hicks, 2014). [Supervisors] need to engage the workforce in figuring this out. The solutions are often going to be in the employees' heads" (Hicks, 2014, p. 2). When engaging employees for solutions and strategic planning, use employee suggestions whenever possible to increase employee morale, which increases employee performance.

Increased supervisory leadership. Many leaders suggested supervisors had one of the most challenging jobs, responsible for the effective of dissemination of information to frontline employees. Supervisors must accurately communicate the organizational mission, vision, and strategy to workers. Given the frequency and detail of information shared, the opportunity for miscommunication was high. Supervisors operated at a disadvantage because they lacked the knowledge and experience of senior leaders (Embry, 2009). U.S. Patent and Trademark Office and National Aeronautics and Space Administration (NASA) were large proponents of supervisory training and development. Both agencies included intensive training for supervisors to assist with developing model supervisors. U.S. Department of State ranked fourth in the 2013 *Best Places to Work in the Federal Government* report, also included training, career development, mentoring, and employee empowerment (Partnership for Public Service, 2013). In each of the agencies highlighted in the Partnership for Public Service report, supervisory training and development were listed as integral to the agencies success with employee performance and morale.

Increased employee engagement. Employee morale is the state of mind or mental condition of an employee. Good employee morale is defined as satisfaction or happiness with the organization. Morale is a component of employee satisfaction (O'Connor, 2006). Employee engagement consists of a heightened connection between workers, their organizations, and their work. Values in employee engagement: pride in work, personal meaning to the work, and a value to the organizations. Six measurable themes identified include (a) pride in one's work, (b) satisfaction with leadership, (c) opportunity to perform well at work, (d) satisfaction with the recognition received, (e) prospect for future growth, and (f) a positive work environment with some focus on teamwork. Employee morale increased when supervisors exhibited positive influence, motivation, inspiration, intellectual opportunities, and concern for the professional needs of employees. To provide morale builders, supervisors must clearly understand the organizational vision, mission, strategies, and goals. Engaged employees took pride in completing their tasks, finding personal meaning in their work, and believing leaders and colleagues within the organization that valued them (Embry, 2009).

U.S. Department of State leaders increased employee engagement by asking employees to come up with new ways to do business and to use social media to communicate "outside its own boundaries" (Partnership for Public Service, 2013, p. 12). NASA encouraged employee engagement with awards programs for innovations, and funding available to employees who wanted to pursue new ideas related to their work (Partnership for Public Service, 2013). The U.S. Department of Transportation (DOT) has an idea hub that is an onsite collection of employee suggestions. Whenever appropriate, DOT implemented the ideas listed on the idea hub. Some implementations included a meeting-room booking system, reduced the number of systems log-ins, and increased the "time required before DOT computers locked employees out of their sessions" (Partnership for Public Service, 2013, p. 15). As shown in the DOT example, often resolving small problems or inconveniences increased employee morale and job satisfaction.

Conclusion

U.S. federal employees worked three years without pay increases, with equipment purchase moratoriums and with hiring freezes or slowdowns. Despite limitations, U.S. federal employees continued to believe in the importance of their work. Through providing annual responses via the *Federal Employee Viewpoint* surveys, U.S. federal employees measured perceptions of the work completed by the agency and satisfaction with the work and the agencies' leaders.

The 2009 Embry study, a mixed-method study at a large U.S. federal agency, examined U.S. federal employee performance and morale. A model presented within the study posited *Increased Supervisory Communication + Increased Supervisory Leadership =*

Increased Employee Engagement created Increased Job Satisfaction + Increased Employee Performance + Decreased Employee Turnover (Embry, 2009).

U.S. federal supervisors at the agency studied in 2009, continued to work toward solutions to increase employee engagement in an effort to decrease employee turnover and to increase employee performance. Supervisors increased communication with employees via meetings, town halls, employee committees, working groups, emails, and other methods. Leaders invested in supervisory training to build model supervisors, and in innovative ideas to improve work processes. Employees responded positively to these actions by increasing the rank of the agency in the Federal Employee Viewport survey (Partnership for Public Service, 2013).

Thoughts from the Academic Entrepreneur™
The problem to be solved:
- U.S. federal employee job satisfaction

The goals:
- To keep government services continuing at the expected level, yet increase U.S. federal employee job satisfaction.

The questions to ask:
- How can one increase job satisfaction when faced with budget cuts, hiring slowdowns, equipment purchase moratoriums, increased worker pension costs, a three-year pay freeze, and a 16-day unpaid furlough?

Today's Business Application:
- Trust and transparency are key, especially in strategic planning. Do not hesitate to communicate the strategic goals of your organization to employees at any level.
- Focus on how you deliver this message, not just the content. Is it believable? Trustworthy? Encouraging?

- Recognize excellent performance from employees, and make sure that this recognition is public and genuine.

References

Brodsky, R., & Newell, E. (2009). Memo to the president-elect. *Government Executive, 41*(1), 25-30.

Colbert, A. (2008). CEO transformational leadership: The role of goal importance congruence in top management teams. *Academy of Management Journal, 51*(1), 81-96.

Embry, S. (2009) *A mixed method study: Understanding employee performance at the Department of Homeland Security* (Doctoral dissertation). (UMI No. 3415962)

Fox, T. (2014, January 2). Tips from U.S. federal agencies with happy employees. *The Washington Post.* Retrieved from http://www.washingtonpost.com/blogs/on-leadership/wp/2014/01/02/tips-from-federal-agencies-with-happy-employees/

Hicks, J. (2014, January 2). U.S. federal workers' tough 2013 is behind them, but they aren't out of the fiscal woods yet. *The Washington Post.* Retrieved from http://www.washingtonpost.com/politics/federal_government/federal-workers-tough-2013-is-behind-them-but-they-arent-out-of-the-fiscal-woods-yet/2014/01/02/5423bc14-73dc-11e3-8def-a33011492df2_story.html

Liberto, J. (2013, June). The U.S. government could soon be facing a shortage of workers. CNN Money. Retrieved January 7, 2014 from http://money.cnn.com/2013/06/13/news/U.S. federal-workers-retire/index.html

Major, D. (2007). Managing human resources: Best practices of high performing supervisors. *Human Resource Management, 46,* 411-427.

O'Connell, M. (November 26, 2013). Satisfied workers key to one small agency's success. *U.S. Federal News Radio.* Retrieved from http://www.U.S.federalnewsradio.com/indenx.pho?nid+851&sid+3513463

O'Connor, T. (2006, September 29). Employee morale (esprit de corps) programs. *Megalinks in Criminal Justice.* Retrieved from http://www.apsu.edu/oconnort/4000/4000lect04.htm

Partnership for Public Service. (2013). *Ten years of the best places to work in the federal government: how six federal agencies improved employee satisfaction and commitment.* Retrieved from http://bestplacestowork.org/BPTW/

rankings/detail/HS17

Rosenberg, A. (2009a, January 26). TSA employees give management low marks. *Government Executive.* Retrieved from http://www.govexec.com/ story_page_pf.cfm?articleid=41875

Rosenberg, A. (2009b). Tapping knowledge. *Government Executive, 41*(1), 16.

Schuttler, R. (2010). *Laws of communication: The intersection where leadership meets employee performance.* Hoboken, NJ: John Wiley & Sons.

Shane, L. (2013, December 19). Sending out an SOS in the workplace rankings. *Government Executive.* Retrieved from http://www.govexec.com/ excellence/promising-practices/2013/12/sending-out-sos-workplace

About the Author...

New York author Dr. Sheila G. Embry holds three accredited degrees: Doctor of Management in Organizational Leadership, Master of Arts in Human Resources Development, and Baccalaureate of Business Administration. She is also a graduate of the Graduate School USA's Executive Potential Program, and a triple graduate of from the U.S. Federal Law Enforcement Training Center.

Dr. Sheila has 22 years' experience with the U.S. federal government working in Buffalo, Denver, El Paso, Kingston, Laguna Niguel, Los Angeles, Louisville, Salt Lake City, Tampa, and Washington, D.C. She has received several professional and community awards.

She is author of 3 Refractive Thinker chapters–

- *Federal Employees and Instructors: Serving the Public Trust*
- *Have We Tipped: Are We Ready to Demand Ethical Behavior from Our Leaders?*
- *The 3Ps of Management: Pushing, Pulling, & Patting*

Articles based on her dissertation include–

- *Communication: The Key to Performance*
- *A Life on (Temporary) Hold: From ABD to DM in 366 days + 3 years*
- *Leadership and Communication: Key Essential to Employee Performance, Morale, Turnover, and Productivity*

Her doctoral study, *A Mixed Method Study: Understanding Employee Performance at The Department of Homeland Security*, provided expertise in supervisory communication effects on employee performance.

To reach Dr. Embry, please check out her blog *Sheila Says* at http://sheilaembry.wordpress.com/

CHAPTER 3

Going Green—Motivating Leaders to Embrace
Environmentally Sustainable Business Practices

By Dr. Danielle J. Camacho and Dr. Jill M. Legare

"Modern technology owes ecology an apology."
Alan M. Eddison

When considering characteristics of strong leaders, an image of a well-spoken, educated person who successfully motivates and leads others might come to mind. Leaders play a critical role in the task of motivating and engaging employees, defining direction and aligning people and resources (Nicholson, 2013). According to Tebeian (2012), a leader is the principal individual who motivates employees to raise performance or change behavior. Motivation is essentially anything that provides direction, intensity and persistence to behavior (Arbak & Villeval, 2013). Leaders play an integral role in change initiatives relating to policy adoption in an organization (Battilana & Casciaro, 2012). Popular theories of motivation include McGregor's (1960) Theory X and Theory Y, and Haefner's (2011) Fourth theory of motivation. Theory X, an authoritarian style of management, posits that the average person dislikes work and is lazy. Leaders following the Theory X style manage employee work with threat of punishment. Conversely, Theory Y allows for a participative style of management. McGregor's Theory Y (1960) describes employees as people who seek and accept responsibility and managers of employees in the role of collaborator or coach. Haefner (2011) described a motivation scheme that included three subsystems- leadership, environment and personalities. The three subsystems were linked by positive core values and systems. In this paper, the authors will provide a refractive thinking perspective on motivating leaders to green the workplace. The goal of this refractive essay is to share literature that outlines specific motivational factors aimed at the ways leaders can make a difference in their workplaces and in the world.

Refractive thinkers must find a way to *motivate* leaders to begin integrating socially responsible practices into business strategies. Prior to performing a formal study, which served as the backdrop for Camacho (2012), *Improving the Environmental Effects of Business Practice Toward Corporate Social Responsibility,* the authors conducted a thorough review of academic literature. Looking to the experts for insight and guidance, a scholarly literature review includes researching a range of motivating factors such as an increase in revenue or positive corporate image as rationale for engaging in responsible business practices. "Doing good for others is a fundamental human value across cultures, employment sectors and typologies of workers" (Belle, 2013, p. 112). Incorporating green actions into strategy seems like common sense and creates a win-win proposition for all stakeholders. However once the discussion turns to 'right' or wrong' the inevitable questions of leadership duties and ethical responsibilities comes to light. Company leaders should behave ethically, and scholars continue to question if we should expect higher standards of company leaders. Lauring and Thomsen (2009) investigated the question of ethics in business noting, "Ethical norms might provide motivation for leaders to consider the output and effects of the products" (p.

27). Advancing the discussion one step further researchers may ask if societal ethics and norms provide 'motivation' for leaders to consider Corporate Social Responsibility (CSR).

Reflecting on the sentinel work of Hardin (1968), the question of the commons becomes the focus of the discussion on responsibility and ethics. Hardin shared, "Freedom in a common brings ruin to all" (1968, p. 1244). Hardin's essay became the launching point for Camacho's (2012) dissertation study. Questions such as--Who is responsible, for what, and to what extent, became the leading questions to frame the research. Andre (2013) argued that company managers have a moral obligation to implement green practice. Although researchers have illustrated the benefits and positive attributes of establishing environmentally responsible practice, leaders of Small and Medium Enterprises (SMEs) might fail to launch green initiatives because of a lack of time, leadership, or personnel.

Going green, corporate social responsibility, and greening of the workplace, these are just a few of the buzzwords that have become part of the language of business in small and large companies alike. Since the 1970s, environmental scientists have been warning leaders about the importance of sustainable practices and keeping the environment 'clean.' Belle (2013) noted, "Inspirational motivation involves articulating a vision of the future that is appealing and inspiring to followers" (p. 110). Transformational leaders can inspire and motivate followers to surpass self- interest for the good of the group. Inspirational leaders, transformational leaders and even transactional leaders are instrumental in motivating stakeholders to embrace environmentally sustainable business practices. Despite the many political, social, and economic pressures, advising leaders to focus on environmentally friendly practices statistics indicate less than 30% of U.S. companies participate in green efforts (U.S. General Services, 2008). CSR refers to the efforts of organizations to implement green practice. Essentially CSR means leaders take steps to incorporate practices that look beyond the scope of the product or service provided—looking holistically at the environmental effect, ways to reduce, reuse, and recycle.

Collectively, Small and Medium Enterprises (SMEs) account for more than 90% of businesses existing within the borders of the United States (Small Business Administration, 2012). A refractive thinker could consider the possibilities if even half of these small business leaders took one-step to green a process in the workplace. Transformational leaders might look at outcomes of a business and decide the worth in making changes to the process for the sake of the community. For example, motivating every small business owner in the U.S. to cancel one domestic airplane trip and instead host a teleconference or video conference would result in savings 4.9 million tons of CO_2 (Kaplan, 2009). The CO_2 savings would translate into approximately 59,529 tanker trucks full of gasoline (Kaplan, 2009).

Strategically going green is a sensible course of action for small business leaders. Leaders at large companies such as Starbucks, IKEA, and Best Buy, for example have posted their sustainability statements and guidelines published on company websites. Leaders of these larger companies could engage SME leaders in discussions of 'what works'-- connecting research from scholars like Zhao (2012) to actual business practices. Lorenzen (2012) noted that green practices should not be viewed as isolated decisions or actions, rather as components in an ongoing project. Researchers have learned that approaching daily operations with a 'business as usual' mindset simply cannot continue—leaders must consider the environmental effects (Angus-Leppan, Metcalf, & Benn, 2010). Despite the large economic presence of SMEs scholars have yet to pinpoint the reasons leaders of small companies have failed 'go green.' Humphreys et al., (2013) argued that instead of small companies failing to engage in green practice, the CSR debate has failed to engage leaders of small business.

Three Components to the Search for What Motivates Leaders to go Green---Economic, Environmental, and Societal Factors— the Triple Bottom Line. Since the early 1970s, scholars have argued that company leaders must look beyond corporate financial goals and instead begin to consider the obligations to protect the environment (Camacho, 2012). Leaders must consider the Triple Bottom Line (TBL)—an approach in which the goals include balancing economic gain, social responsibility, and protection of the environment (Elkington, 2006).

Positive corporate image motivates leaders of well-known companies such as Intel, Dupont, Nike, or Ikea to embrace green processes. Tang, Hull, and Rothenberg (2012) described the importance of company image as a motivating factor for incorporating green practices. Claydon (2011) noted customer pressure, legislation and individual concerns as primary reasons leaders of companies will initiate sustainability strategies in the organization. Other companies will align processes with green actions because of the requirements of key buyers (Lee, 2009). Motivating leaders to embrace green practice is no simple task. General Motors and Honda Motors, for example required vendors to adhere to green standards in their procurement procedure-- companies wishing to maintain business relations with these partners, must find methods to adhere to both environmental regulations and customer requirements.

Haefner's (2011) Fourth Theory of Motivation emphasized the importance of leaders driving and motivating employees by establishing guiding principles and maintaining core values. Integrating green practices requires more than simply taking steps to exceed the 'regulatory' requirements—by incorporating one or two green processes into the company practices. Scholars described the availability of resources, owner interest and financial consequences as key elements that can influence the decision to go green. Baumann-Pauly, Wickert, Spence, and Scherer (2013), posited that leaders must find a way to link CSR not only to the strategy but throughout the value chain in the organization. Sustainability must be integrated into the corporate strategy—it cannot be isolated from the organization's vision. Trends indicate that companies continue to embrace the social obligation to implement green practices and that whether the organization benefits financially from integrating green practices is only partly relevant (Marcus & Fremeth, 2009). Leaders are responsible for instituting behaviors that create core values, core values that encourage positive change.

Introducing . . . Life Cycle Analysis (LCA)

Employees are greatest asset of a workforce—leaders should continue to train and develop employees. McGregor's Theory Y (1960) described a management style in which leaders trust workers, empowering an intrinsically motivated workforce. Refractive thinkers can imagine the pride of workmanship and creative solutions that become possible when employees are motivated to craft solutions. Employees who are free from the barriers such as fear of retaliation for unwelcomed comments and who can suggest creative solutions are instrumental in reviewing company practices, which require insight and a fresh perspective (Haefner, 2011). One creative method to address the Triple Bottom Line (TBL) goals (economic, social and environmental) is to consider the life cycle of a given process. A refractive thinker could illustrate the TBL goals in a review of the life cycle of a pair of shoes. An LCA-minded shoe manufacturer, for example, would focus attention on the life cycle of a shoe from the raw material extraction to the manufacturing cycle, and then from transportation to possible reutilization or disposal. Leaders can apply Life Cycle Management (LCM) into the workplace to transform work processes to become more friendly to the environment. LCM is a management approach that incorporates the entire life cycle of a product—from cradle to grave (Keen, 2012). By means of example, leaders of Nike, thinking outside the proverbial box, created a reuse a shoe program and working with the city of Tucson, AZ. Employees from Nike collected and recycled shoes that became the padding for basketball courts (Petru, 2011). Like the initiative at Nike, Camacho (2012) investigated possibilities of reducing or reusing materials in the life cycle.

The Study

Linking theory to practice, Camacho (2012) investigated factors that motivate leaders of SMEs to green organizational practice. Scholars rely on one type of green action, Life Cycle Analysis (LCA) to learn the steps that needed to incorporate green practices into small companies. Camacho centered on answering four research questions, with the goal of understanding the motivation and communication that would result in green practices.

The findings in this case study related to the following four research questions:
  1. What steps are needed to implement LCA into SMEs?
  2. What are the costs incurred with LCA integration?
  3. What are the savings achieved with integration of LCA?
  4. What strategies and solutions can SMEs
     use to transform their organizations into
     green entities?, (Camacho, 2012, p. 15)

Literature reviewed from the 1970s to 2013 included arguments for and against green practices founded in cost, social norms, and ecology. Epstein's (2008) CSM theory provided the backdrop to create a systematic approach for integrating LCA into a SME. Leaders addressing CSR opportunities for a small company must focus on the causes, effects, and underlying interactions. The CSM framework provides perspective for leaders to address environmental, social and economic factors.

Because of the scarcity of literature on life cycle analysis, Camacho (2012) focused on greening efforts in a given life cycle. The direction and focus of the study was driven by the presence of literature on CSR and the absences of research addressing Life Cycle Analysis and SMEs. The success of LCA requires the establishment of clear boundaries, determining the input and output during a process, and identifying the process that results in the greatest reduction of waste and resources.

Summary of Themes

The themes discovered in Camacho's (2012) research were not surprising; instead, the themes remind leaders that strategy, motivation and communication persist as the underlying ingredients required for establishing and maintaining competitive positions. Laudal (2011) suggested a lack of knowledge in the workplace regarding green practice. Leaders must become the driving force of the green process. Leaders should establish guiding principles, core values and motivate employees to excel in green pursuits (Haefner, 2011). SMEs must create clear policies about going green and construct an active education programs for all stakeholders. The information gathered from the research study was used to highlight a gap between the desire of leaders to green the organization and the incentives for both the employer and employees to take steps toward green work processes. According to the findings, an opportunity exists for SMEs to partner with general contractors or larger firms to share the costs and responsibilities associated with green initiatives on construction sites. Research related to initiatives implemented toward CSR within SMEs must continue. There is a need for a clearer understanding of specific characteristics affecting the ability of leaders within any given organization to go green.

Recommendations for Action

Opportunities exist for leaders of SMEs to take action toward green operation of their organizations. The integration of LCA provides a holistic overview of the environmental effects of business activities, allowing leaders to assess the environmental trade-offs of their decisions (Su, Zhang, & Yuan, 2010). Opportunities toward effective green operation include creating and communicating clear policy on green practice; educating employees; and partnering with customers, clients, and the community opportunities toward effective green operation. The CSM developed by Epstein (2008) focused on three initiatives—economic gain, social responsibility, and protection of the environment. Epstein reported improved long- term shareholder returns, increased ability to strategically plan, and reduced operating costs after implementing CSM.

Theme 1: Lack of Incentives to Motivate Employees

Lack of Motivation--In the absence of 'clear' incentives to engage in the practice, leaders and employees alike will not engage in green practices. The decision to engage in CSR activities is a strategic choice. Leaders who take steps to integrate LCA into daily business practice must consider the corporate culture embedded within their business operations. Researchers have described the need for creating green options for businesses and a need for additional resources to educate employees (Tang et al.,

2012). Whereas some SME leaders believe CSR initiatives take too much time and potential positive results remain insignificant (Hidayati, 2011), others approach the challenge of greening their organizations with optimism (Crittenden, Crittenden, Ferrell, Ferrell, & Pinney, 2011). As employees do not fully understand the best methods of greening work processes, leaders must embed green practices and processes into the corporate culture. By defining clear goals for green action, both employers and employees can understand the incentives to participate in green work processes. Motivating employees to move toward *green practices,* Epstein (2008) suggested a need to establish a defined reward system as precursory to launching an effective CSR program. Employees revealed they would participate in green actions if compensated for the work time (e.g., driving time and time invested in breaking down cardboard boxes), or if the actions did not adversely affect the time expended on their work (Camacho, 2012).

Theme 2: Need for Education- Communication

To launch a successful CSR program, it is necessary to write and distribute expectations and company policies regarding going green. In addition, managers can construct active education programs that communicate education on the CSR opportunities, policies and adopted company practices. SMEs must translate CSR initiatives into a formal management system (Russo & Perrini, 2010). Fassin, VanRossem, and Bulens (2011) reported that employees with high levels of awareness become more inclined to participate in green initiatives. Although SMEs might embrace informal language and communication, scholars suggested creating a clear policy and documenting training materials to help engage employees in prescribed green actions such as recycling or reusing materials (Tang et al., 2012). The adoption of voluntary green practice requires employee commitment and forward thinking by management. To gain buy in, green initiatives must be practical and actionable. Green policies and practice can be created as a guide for managerial practice whenever possible (Luu, 2013). Leaders can take action to green their organizations by creating policy grounded in green practice. SME leaders must also educate employees, and CSR initiatives must align with corporate strategies (Raska & Shaw, 2012). Following the prescribed actions shared in Theme 2, leaders of SMEs can heighten employee awareness and foster a culture conducive to implementing green practice.

Theme 3: Opportunity for Partnership

SMEs can collaborate with general contractors or larger firms to share the costs and responsibilities associated with green initiatives on construction sites. While sustainability initiatives start at one end of the supply chain and end with the customer, each stakeholder has a valuable role to play in the process (Baumann-Pauly et al., 2013). Camacho (2012) focused on cradle-to-grave actions. Cradle-to-grave reviews allow leaders to track the life cycle of a product from the point of creation until disposal of the product. The study site investigated did not manufacture the components required to complete construction jobs (Camacho, 2012), leading to a finding that creates an opportunity for partnership between the purchasing company and the external vendors supplying job-related materials. By collaborating with vendors, participating organizations enjoy a mutually beneficial partnership that addresses goals identified by LCA. The need exists for construction companies to form partnerships toward the reduction of waste and an increase in green work processes (Sethi, Veral, Shapiro, & Emelianova, 2011). Some construction companies provide separate containers on work sites for trash, drywall, metal, wood, and glass. Green measures can be instituted through formal initiatives that meet Leadership in Energy and Environmental Design (LEED) certification requirements or partially fulfill an organizational commitment to green the workplace. Regardless of motive, the need exists for recycling practice on construction job sites. Refractive thinkers suggest partnering with general contractors or the private parties responsible for the construction, leaders of SMEs can negotiate trash and recycling requirements. CSR actions create goodwill and will increase the number of items recycled in lieu of dumpster disposal. Leaders of SMEs can accomplish green goals by forming partnerships with customers, clients, and the community.

Themes and Patterns

Research question (RQ)	Themes	Patterns
RQ1: What steps are needed to implement LCA into SMEs?	Need for education; need for partnership with larger firms; lack of incentive to partici-pate	Lack of initiative to going green; no incentive toward green processes
RQ2: What are the costs in-curred with LCA integration?	Manpower costs; sup-ply costs; costs related to time away from job site; consultant time	Cost prohibitive to green processes
RQ3: What are the savings achieved with integration of LCA?	Time spent away from job site; reduced waste; im-proved morale	Little monetary incentive to green processes; no return on investment
RQ4: What strategies and solutions can SMEs use to transform their organizations into green entities?	Partnership with gen-eral contractors; clear policies on going green and active education program	Possibility to partner with contractors; concern over the incentive to partner

Summary and Study Conclusions

This essay is brief review of the opportunities for leaders to serve as catalysts in launching green practices. Every type of leader—from transactional, transformational, servant leaders, managers, supervisors, lead employee –and every team member can play a role in greening the workplace. Corporate practices, societal norms and law describe the obligation that leaders of these organizations have that extends beyond the financial goals of maximizing wealth (Andre, 2013). Motivating leaders to embrace green practices is paramount to corporate survival (Valackiene & Miceviciene, 2011). The business case for motivating leaders to incorporate CSR is that green practice benefits stakeholders and creates a corporate culture wherein participants become vested in sustainability. Given time, financing, and resources, all companies can institute change toward environmental improvement, whether large or small changes. As there is significant potential for leaders to embrace green practices, refractive thinkers must find a way to motivate leaders to begin integrating socially responsible practices into business strategies. Leaders of SMEs must review their business practice and policies to create a program addressing gaps. Moving forward will require that leaders support the advancement of life-cycle thinking. Continued research and the application of refractive thinking in the field might result in a clear link between theory and the practical application of green practice. Leaders have the opportunity to create policies, practices and corporate cultures that motivate employees to embrace green practices—practices that will significantly reduce the effects of business activities on the environment.

Thoughts from the Academic Entrepreneur™
The problem to be solved:
- Integrating socially responsible practices into business strategies

The goals:
- Researching a range of motivating factors such as an increase in revenue or positive corporate image as

rationale for engaging in responsible business practices

The questions to ask:

- Can [Or how do?] societal ethics and norms provide 'motivation' for leaders to consider Corporate Social Responsibility?

Today's Business Application

- Understand and absorb the concept of a triple bottom line, and make sure that your management team understands what a triple bottom line is as well.
- Conduct a Life Cycle Analysis (LCA) of the company's products, and investigate how the process could be made environmentally sustainable.
- Motivate employees with clear incentives to adopt green, sustainable processes, and encourage *out of the box* suggestions from workers at all levels of your organization.

References

Arbak, E., & Villeval, M. (2013). Voluntary leadership: Motivation and influence. *Social Choice and Welfare, 40*(3), 635-662. doi:10.1007/s00355-011-0626-2

André, K. (2013). The ethics of care as a determinant for stakeholder inclusion and CSR perception in business education. *Society and Business Review, 8*(1), 32-44. doi:10.1108/17465681311297667

Angus-Leppan, T., Metcalf, L., & Benn, S. (2010). Leadership styles and CSR practice: An examination of sense making, institutional drivers and CSR leadership. *Journal of Business Ethics, 93*(2), 189-213. doi:10.1007/s10551-009-0221-y

Baumann-Pauly, D., Wickert, C., Spence, L. J., & Scherer, A. G. (2013). Organizing corporate social responsibility in small and large firms: Size matters. *Journal of Business Ethics,* 115, 693-705. doi:10.1007/s10551-013-1827-7

Battilana, J., & Casciaro, T. (2012). Change agents, networks, and institutions: A contingency theory of organizational change. *Academy of Management Journal, 55,* 381-398.

Bellé, N. (2014). Leading to make a difference: A field experiment on the performance effects of transformational leadership, perceived social impact, and public service motivation. *Journal of Public Administration Research & Theory, 24*(1), 109-136

Camacho, D. J. (2012). *Improving the environmental effects of business practice toward corporate social responsibility* (Doctoral dissertation). Retrieved from ProQuest Dissertations and Theses database. (UMI No. 3498379)

Claydon, J. (2011). A new direction for CSR: The shortcomings of previous CSR models and the rationale for a new model. *Social Responsibility Journal, 7,* 405-420. doi:10.1108/17471111111154545

Crittenden, V. L., Crittenden, W. F., Ferrell, L. K., Ferrell, O. C., & Pinney, C. C. (2011). Market-oriented sustainability: A conceptual framework and propositions. *Academy of Marketing Science. Journal, 39*(1), 71-85. doi:10.1007/s11747-010-0217-2

Elkington, J. (2006). *The triple bottom line.* In M. J. Epstein & K. O. Hanson (Eds.), *The accountable corporation* (Vol. 3, pp. 97–110). Westport, CT: Prager.

Epstein, M. J. (2008). *Making sustainability work: Best practices in managing and measuring corporate social, environmental, and economic impacts.* San Francisco, CA: Berrett-Koehler.

Fassin, Y., Van Rossem, A., & Bulens, M. (2011). Small-business owner-managers' perceptions on business ethics and CSR-Related concepts. *Journal of Business Ethics, 98,* 425–453. doi:10.1007/s10551-010-0586-y

Haefner, J. J. (2011). The fourth theory of worker motivation. *Industrial Management, 53*(2), 17.

Hardin, G. (1968). The tragedy of the commons. *Science,* 162, 1243–1248.

Hidayati, N. (2011). Pattern of corporate social responsibility programs: A case study. *Social Responsibility Journal, 7*(1), 104–117. doi:10.1108/17471111111114576

Humphreys, J. H., Haden, S. P., Hayek, M., Einstein, J., Fertig, J., Paczkowski, W., & Weir, D. (2013). Entrepreneurial stewardship and implicit CSR: The responsible leadership of Lillian Shedd McMurry. *Journal of Applied Management and Entrepreneurship, 18*(3), 25-50.

Keen, M. (2012). Managing the supply chain contribution at various points along the product life cycle. *Management Services, 56*(1), 14-16.

Laudal, T. (2011). Drivers and barriers of CSR and the size and internationalization of firms. *Social Responsibility Journal, 7,* 234–256. doi:10.1108/17471111111141512

Lauring, J., & Thomsen, C. (2009). Ideals and practices in CSR identity making: The case of equal opportunities. Employee Relations, *31*(1), 25-38. doi:10.1108/01425450910916805

Lee, K. H. (2009). Why and how to adopt green management into business organizations? *Management Decision, 47,* 1101–1121. doi:10.1002/csr.239

Lorenzen, J. A. (2012). Going green: The process of lifestyle change. *Sociological Forum, 27*(1), 94-116. doi:10.1111/j.1573-7861.2011.01303.x

Luu, T. T. (2013). Corporate social responsibility, upward influence behavior, team processes and competitive intelligence. *Team Performance Management, 19*(1), 6-33. Doi:10.1108/13527591311312079

Marcus, A., & Fremeth, A. (2009). Green management matters regardless. *Academy of Management Perspectives, 7,* 17–26. doi:10.1111/j.1467-6486.2010.00993.x

Nicholson, N. (2013). Engaging leadership - the Duke Ellington way. *Strategic HR Review, 12,* 322-323.

Petru, A. (2011). *Nike to recycle shoes into playgrounds. Retrieved* from http://earth911.com/news/2011/10/14/nike-to-recycle-shoes-into-playgrounds/

Raska, D., & Shaw, D. (2012). When is going green good for company image? Management Research Review, 35, 326-347. doi:10.1108/01409171211210190

Sethi, S. S., Veral, E., Shapiro, H. H., & Emelianova, O. (2011). Mattel, Inc.: Global manufacturing principles (GMP)-A life-cycle analysis of a company-based code of conduct in the toy industry. *Journal of Business Ethics, 99,* 483-517. doi:10.1007/s10551-010-0673-0

Small Business Administration (SBA). (2012). Advocacy: The voice of small business in government. Retrieved from http://www.sba.gov/sites/default/files/FINAL%20FAQ%202012%20Sept%202012%20web.pd

Su, X., Zhang, X., & Yuan, Y. (2010). Environmental performance of power generation system in China based on LCA. *AIP Conference Proceedings, 1251*(1), 260-263. doi:10.1063/1.3529294

Tang, Z., Hull, C., & Rothenberg, S. (2012). How corporate social responsibility engagement strategy moderates the CSR-financial performance relationship. *Journal of Management Studies, 49*(7), 1274-1303. doi:10.1111/j.1467-6486.2012.01068.x

Tebeian A. (2012). How to improve employee motivation and group performance through leadership-Conceptual Model. *Annals of The University Of Oradea, Economic Science Series,* 2192-1097.

U.S. General Services. (2008.) *Sustainable design program.* Retrieved from http://www. gsa.gov/Portal/gsa/ep/contentView.do?contentType=GSA_OVERVIEW&content Id=8154&noc=T

Valackiene, A., & Miceviciene, D. (2011). Methodological framework analysing a social phenomenon: Stakeholder orientation implementing balanced corporate social responsibility. *Engineering Economics, 22,* 300-308.

Zhao, M. (2012). CSR-based political legitimacy strategy: Managing the state by doing good in china and russia. *Journal of Business Ethics, 111,* 439-460. doi:10.1007/s10551-012-1209-6

About the Author...

Dr. Danielle J. Camacho resides in Gilbert, Arizona. Dr. Camacho holds several accredited degrees; a Bachelor of Arts (BA) in Psychology from Baylor University; a Master of Business Administration (MBA) from the University of Dallas, and a Doctorate of Business Administration (DBA) from Walden University.

Dr. Danielle is an Adjunct Faculty Member at Upper Iowa University, approved to teach business and management courses. She enjoys coaching and mentoring students in the online classroom. Dr. Danielle is a member of the Alpha Phi Omega Fraternity and the Society of Human Resources Management (SHRM).

Her doctoral study, *Improving the Environmental Effects of Business Practice Toward Corporate Social Responsibility*, provided Dr. Danielle the opportunity to gain professional and academic expertise to facilitate green initiatives within a small company in the construction industry.

To reach Dr. Camacho for information on consulting or doctoral coaching, please e-mail: daniellejcamacho@gmail.com

About the Author...

Dr. Jill M. Legare resides in Chicago IL. Dr. Jill holds several accredited degrees; a Bachelor of Arts (BA) in Journalism from Baylor University; a Master of Arts in History (MA) from Claremont Graduate University, a Masters of Business Administration (MBA) from Keller Graduate School and a Doctorate in Educational Leadership (EDd) from Argosy University.

Dr. Jill is an Adjunct faculty member at the Art Institutes, Excelsior College and DeVry University, approved to teach history, business, management, and English courses. Her goal in the online classroom is to promote life-long learning, diversity and ethics in the online classroom.

To reach Dr. Legare for information on consulting or doctoral coaching, please e-mail: jlxrugby@aol.com

CHAPTER 4

Five Steps to Navigating the Social Exchange Perspective Landscape

By Dr. Ernest Jones

Leaders seeking to implement organizational interventions face many challenges. Interruptions, competing priorities, and complex interconnectedness can inhibit not only managerial effectiveness but also the manager's ability to motivate team members. Jones (2013) conducted a mixed methods exploration into one such potential source of complex interconnectedness. Operationalized as social exchange perspective, the Jones study investigated the holistic viewpoints on social exchange constructs held by individuals working in a participatory process. Leaders are encouraged to use the varied social exchange perspectives within organizations to develop effective organizational interventions. By acknowledging and appreciating diversity of social exchange perspective—the social exchange perspective landscape—leaders can align and orient internal motivation to implement sustainable interventions with high levels of buy-in.

Why Explore Social Exchange Perspective

Manz and Sims (1980) stressed the importance of self-managing behaviors. Self-managing behaviors, as defined by the Manz and Sims, are actions indicative of internal motivation. At its core, the notion of self-managing behavior presumes that any increase in the expression of internally held motivation is good for the organization. However, a wholesale increase in self-managing actions might not have its intended effect.

Kankanhali et al. (2006) investigated factors affecting work team performance and provides another reason for exploring social exchange perspective. The model suggests that in addition to task complexity and task interdependence, relationship quality is a moderator of performance. Although task conflict and functional diversity were seen as potentially positive within virtual work teams, relationship conflict was found by Kankanhali et al. to be detrimental in all studied cases. Therefore, managers should understand the sources of relationship conflict among the organizational membership.

Senge (1990) espoused that part of the role of leadership is to surface and address mental models. Mental models are the underlying ontological and epistemological assumptions that permeate an organization. Senge asserts, as a primary skill, the ability to eliminate mental models with negative self-reinforcing characteristics while instilling, exposing, and replicating mental models with positive self-reinforcing characteristics.

The social exchange perspective landscape is asserted as the manifestation of a mental models. A subjective viewpoint on social exchanges held by individuals within an organization, social exchange perspective, according to Jones (2013), is indicative of working relationship quality. Using sales and operations planning (S&OP) as a managerial context, Jones built a conceptual framework around what S&OP participants think about working relationships and subsequent willingness to participate in the S&OP process.

Sales and Operations Planning

S&OP or integrated business planning, is a cross-functional process usually facilitated by supply chain managers within manufacturing and service organizations (Palmatier & Crum, 2002). The process provides a linkage between a long-term business plan and short-term tactical plans. The limited scholarly literature about S&OP indicated that, although the S&OP process is robust and optimal from a management science perspective, the reality is that implementation results are inconsistent. S&OP is a logical succession of meetings designed to ensure internal coordination of internal value chain functions. Grimson and Pyke (2007) described S&OP as a process through which leaders survey the organization's external environment, develop an estimate of future demand, assess internal capabilities, and identify gaps between supply and demand. The gaps are escalated for tradeoff decision-making by senior management. The process, typically facilitated by supply chain professionals, includes individuals from each organizational function.

Jones (2013) asserted that the success of an S&OP process could be a result of participatory behaviors exhibited by cross-functional S&OP team members. Additionally, Jones propositioned that the participatory behaviors of individual teams members could be influenced by an individual's viewpoint on working relationships. The resulting conceptual framework was a dialectical argument proposing: a) what people think about working relationships (i.e. social exchange perspective) influences and is influenced by participatory behavior (i.e. S&OP participation) and, b) the quality of S&OP participation influences and is influenced by S&OP process outputs and outcomes.

Relevant Literature

Jones (2013) relied on two bodies of knowledge. Social exchange theoretical constructs were used to build a model of social exchange perspective formulation. Social exchange perspective was operationalized as the subjective stance an individual takes upon considering his or her own feelings toward social exchanges. Self-managing behavioral constructs were used to build a model of S&OP participation.

Theories of social exchange have a rich history and are the subject of a large body of academic literature. Jones (2013) used Engestrom's (1987) activity systems modeling to operationalize the concept of social exchange perspective formulation. The formulation of social exchange perspective was theorized as the output of an activity system that accounts for social rules (e.g. reciprocity norms, fairness and justice, normative commitment). Jones proposed social exchange perspective is produced through exchange beliefs (e.g. perceived organizational support and continuance commitment) and distributed through exchange intentions, a construct comprised of affective commitment, organizational citizenship intent, satisfaction, trust, and withdrawal intent.

The participatory behavior literature is similarly broad and rich. Again, Jones (2013) used activity systems modeling to operationalize S&OP participation as the object of an individual operating cross-functionally. Dyadic exchange quality with leaders, coworkers, functional teams, and project teams, according to Jones' model, mediates participation. Participatory behavior is distributed through self-managing actions, self-effort, and delegated effort. Additionally, participatory behavior was theorized as produced through self-managing leader behavior (i.e. an individual's perception of how much he is encouraged by leadership to use self-managing actions).

Method

The research design was a dominant qualitative study was completed in parallel with a quantitative survey. The social exchange perspectives landscape was assessed using Q-methodology (McKeown & Thomas, 1988; Watts & Stenner, 2012). Q-methodology was appropriate because its technique can objectively handle the highly subjective nature of an individual's perception of social exchanges. For the qualitative portion of the study, 32 participants completed a q-sort describing their current work situation within the context of validated social exchange items previously published by Eisenberger et al. (2001).

Sixty additional participants completed a survey comprised of not only self-managing behavioral items published in Uhl-Bien (1991), but also the Eisenberger et al. (2001) items used in the qualitative portion of the study. Danielson's (2009) profile correlation technique was used to detect social exchange perspective in the survey data set. Finally, analysis of variance (ANOVA) was used to test for associations among social exchange perspectives and self-managing behavioral constructs.

Findings

The q-method portion of study indicated four factors representing the collective patterns of thought held by study participants within the context of social exchanges. Upon close analysis, the findings suggest one prevailing belief and three attitudinal dimensions held among S&OP participants. The quantitative portion of the study showed statistically significant associations among social exchange perspective and participatory constructs including leader-member exchange, functional member exchange, S&OP-team member exchange, and job problems.

The Internally Motivated Achiever

The *internally motivated achiever* is a common belief held among the study participants (Jones, 2013). This viewpoint is characterized by a strong sense of felt obligation to the organization. According to Jones, adherents to the internally motivated achiever perspective believe:

- I owe it to my organization to do whatever I can to ensure our customers are well served and satisfied
- I continue to look for new ways to improve the effectiveness of my work
- I owe it to my organization to give 100% of my energy to the organization's goals while I'm at work
- I feel a personal obligation to do whatever I can to help my organization achieve its goals

Jones (2013) also found that *internally motivated achievers* do not feel:

- My organization really cares about my well-being
- An employee who is treated badly by a company should work less hard
- I feel that the only obligation I have to my organization is to fulfill the minimum requirement for my job

Internally motivated achievers tend to exhibit a high use of self-managing actions. Adherents to the perspective are encouraged by management to express self-managing actions. Individuals with this perspective tend to maintain effective working relationships and these employees usually view job problems (structural problems within the organizational culture) as no more than minor issues.

An Attitudinal Dimension based on Support and Satisfaction

Support and satisfaction comprised the strongest attitudinal factor. Jones (2013) found the *supported and satisfied performer* viewpoint believe:

- My organization values my contributions to its well-being
- I feel a strong sense of belonging to my organization
- My organization strongly considers my goals and values
- Most of the time, I am satisfied with my job
- My organization takes pride in my accomplishments
- I feel emotionally attached to my organization

Adherents to the *supported and satisfied performer* perspective reject the notions that:

- I intend on beginning work on time
- Employees should not care about the organization that employs them unless that organization shows that it cares about its employees
- My attendance at meetings is above the norm
- I am not eager to change my job, but I would do so if I could get a better job

Supported and satisfied performers (21% of study participants) maintain good working relationships but do not take steps to improve working relationships. Adherents to this perspective tend to actively seek new on-the-job experiences for self-improvement and are least likely to report the existence of job problems.

On the other side of this attitudinal dimension is the *unsupported and unsatisfied non-performer* archetype whose profile is opposite of its bi-polar converse. Namely, adherents to this perspective (11% of study participants) have low perceived organizational support, low job satisfaction, are highly likely to change jobs, and have little affective commitment to the organization. Behaviorally, *unsupported and unsatisfied non-performers* report low levels of trust, low levels of closeness with co-workers, and an inability to rely on the co-worker expertise. Adherents see lack of upward mobility and managerial competence as major organizational problems.

An Attitudinal Dimension Based on Individual and Manager Focus

A second attitudinal dimension focuses on the individual and the manager. The *self-focused non-performer* archetype is characterized by an imbalance toward what might be gained from the organizations over what could be provided to the organization. Adherents to this perspective believe:

- My organization is willing to help me if I need a special favor
- I owe it to my organization to do what I can to ensure that our customers are well-served and satisfied
- An employee's work effort should depend partly on how well the organization deals with his or her desires and concerns
- I feel that the only obligation I have to my organization is to fulfill the minimum requirements for my job

Self-focused non-performers, according to Jones (2013), reject the notions that:

- I feel a personal obligation to do whatever I can to help my organization achieve its goals
- I strive to be cheerful at work
- I have an obligation to my organization to ensure that I produce high quality work

- I enjoy discussing my organization with people who do not work here
- I assist my manager with his or her work

Self-focused non-performers (6% of study participants) tend to have low energy and are not likely to be helpful to their managers. The study sample, unfortunately, was not sufficient to fully articulate the participatory behaviors expressed by this archetype.

The *manager-focused performer* attitude, conversely, tends to focus on the value provided to one's direct manager. This archetype tends to express high energy and maintain better than average working relationships with S&OP members. One drawback of this perspective (11% of study participants) is that *manager-focused performer* archetype prioritizes manager needs before customer needs.

A Final Attitudinal Dimension based on Altruism and Reward

A third attitudinal dimension juxtaposes altruism with reward centricity. The *altruistic low performer* archetype (8% of study participants) seems to operate within the rules of selflessness. However, this archetype's intentions are not helpful to either coworkers or to the functioning of the work group. *Altruistic low performers* are willing to give personal time to help the organization when requested and are not likely to feel guilty if performance standards are not met. Conversely, *reward-minded strong performers* are highly attuned to the balance of exchange. Jones (2013) found that *reward-minded strong performers* think:

- An employee should only work hard if his or her efforts will lead to a pay increase, promotion, or other benefits
- An employee who is treated badly by a company should work less hard

- I would feel guilty if I did not meet my organization's performance standards
- I perform the tasks that are expected of me
- I help coworkers who have been absent

The results of the study also found that adherents to *the reward minded strong performer* attitude reject notions that:

- I would feel an obligation to take time from my personal schedule to help my organization if it needed my help
- Employees should only go out of their way to help their organization if it goes out of its way to help them
- If an organization does not appreciate an employee's efforts, the employee should still work as hard as he or she can
- An employee's work effort should not depend on the fairness of his or her pay
- Duties assigned to me are completed adequately
- Employees should work as hard as possible no matter what the organization thinks of his or her efforts
- I am not eager to change my job, but I would do so if I could get a better job

Adherents to the *reward-minded strong performer* perspective set high performance standards for themselves, would feel guilty if performance standards are not met, are helpful to absent coworkers, and are not eager to leave the organization. The problem is the *reward-minded strong performers* (8% of study participants) are likely to be exceptional individual contributors but poor team players.

Implications and Recommendations

The overarching research questions driving the Jones (2013) study were:

- What are the prevailing social exchange perspectives held among S&OP participants?
- What are the participatory behaviors expressed by S&OP participants?
- How does participatory behavior change based on the social exchange perspectives held?

Jones assessed both what participants think about the health of their working relationships and what participants are likely to do as adherents to attitudes within the perspective landscape. The perspective landscape, surfaced in the study, includes one commonly held belief and three distinct attitudinal dimensions.

Implications for Theory Testing

Jones (2013) suggested that paradigm-shifting studies within the social exchange extant literature are in the form of conceptual essays proposing new constructs, confirmatory factor analyses investigating concept distinctiveness, or structural equation models investigating construct cause-effect pathways. By using q-methodology rather than the typically used quantitative techniques, the study extended the social exchange literature and demonstrated the effectiveness of q-methodology for theory testing. The support and satisfaction dimension aligns closely with the model of perceived organizational support and affective commitment espoused by Eisenberger et al. (2001). The altruism-reward archetype also aligns closely with the model of generalized and negotiated reciprocity espoused by Molm (2010).

Implications for Future Research

Participant incidence was a challenge to study completion (Jones, 2013). The quantitative portion of the study involved using a business-to-business (B2B) panel at a rather exorbitant cost per response. Cost limited the size of the quantitative sample and, subsequently, limited the statistical power of the quantitative analysis. Researchers seeking to leverage the study's research design could consider two alternatives.

One alternative is to consider gathering data from a small number of organization cases. Benefits include the opportunity for case comparisons and the possibility to extend the conceptual framework to include the functioning of the participatory process. An organizational-centric research design was not proposed because of the potentially sensitive nature of the social exchange theories under investigation. Participant anonymity could be better protected with the individual-centric design thereby yielding more candid results especially from individuals with high withdrawal intent or low job satisfaction.

Changing the managerial context is a second alternative for continued research. S&OP was chosen specifically because the process relates to daily work of supply chain professionals. However, the population is relatively small and somewhat difficult to access. The study's conceptual model could be fit to many participative processes such as professional service work groups, geographically distributed virtual work team, senior leadership teams, or non-profit boards of directors. On balance, focusing on the S&OP managerial context was deemed important because the process itself is espoused by professional trade associations as the gold standard or best practice. Yet, process effectiveness varies dramatically from organization to organization. Typical writings on the S&OP process are either normative theories of practice based on idealized case study or the summarized results of numerical optimization studies. Conversely, the Jones (2013) study focused on the human element involved in the participatory process. The study embraces what cannot be accounted for in optimizations and has not been accounted for fully in the available S&OP academic literature. At its core, the findings provide support for the notion that the social exchange perspective landscape moderates participatory process effectiveness.

Implications for Practice

One notable finding is that self-managing actions—behaviors indicative of intrinsic motivation—are not statistically associated with social exchange perspective (Jones, 2013). Participants indicated frequent engagement in self-diagnosis, self-monitoring and self-directed goal setting regardless not only of exchange quality with coworkers and leaders but also regardless of social exchange perspective. The research indicated no statistically significant differences between social exchange perspective and self-managing leader behavior—the degree that individuals are encouraged by leadership to engage in self-managing actions. However, participants believe management's propensity to encourage use of self-managing actions is less than the propensity of the participants themselves to use self-managing actions.

At first glance, a quick win for leaders seems to emerge if leaders encourage the organization to use self-managing actions, then the organization reaps positive outcomes. The problem, however, is that adherents to both the performing and non-performing viewpoints engage in self-management to the statistically same degree. Unfortunately, an increase in self-managing actions might not be conducive to the functioning of the organization.

Implications for Organizational Interventions

The use of study's method—namely, the segmentation of organizational members along patterns of thought—has important managerial implications. Jones (2013) found that, although the *internally motivated achiever* archetype is the commonly held belief among S&OP participants, 75% of the organization is likely to also adhere to one of three attitudinal dimensions. Without an understanding of social exchange perspective landscape found in the study and, more importantly, the perspective landscape within specific organizations, managers are at risk of generating negative unintended outcomes.

Recommendations

Managers could presume organizations have static cultures that cannot be influenced. However, this *do-nothing* approach has drawbacks. Similarly, the opposite extreme, where management adopts Senge's (1990) espousal to seek out and address adherents to non-performing viewpoints, might not be productive. One could argue for seeking out non-performing archetypes and surfacing the critical few within the organization representing the greatest inhibitor to organization performance. But such an organization still fails to acknowledge that the remaining three quarters of its members have four distinct modes of thought and behavior. Moreover, the very act of seeking out non-performing viewpoints, could have an impact on the perspective landscape itself as some members of the organization could regard such management activity in a pejorative light.

The preferred alternative is drawn from Cuppen's (2010) constructive conflict approach. the method embraces the perspective landscape and seeks to surface each viewpoint's inherent strengths. The five steps to navigating the perspective landscape are:

1. Segment based on perspective
2. Engage and understand issues
3. Ask for a fix
4. Evaluate and improve using divergent perspectives
5. Decide and implement (Cuppen, 2010).

The q-methodological approach can be used to identify the diversity of thought based on a specific issue within the organization. Jones (2013) used theories of social exchange to assess social exchange perspectives held among S&OP participants. However, additional discourses and concourses could be relevant. For instance, an organization seeking to improve its supply chain performance could assess varied perspectives on the current state of supply chain practices by evaluating q-sorts based on established best practices. Leaders seeking to increase the use of technology among virtual work teams could use a concourse built from theories of technology adoption rate, knowledge transfer, and work team communication.

Once the perspective landscape is known, the next step is to engage the membership to understand the issues. Leaders could conduct small focus groups or intensive interviews among likeminded individuals. The goal of the sessions are to gain better insight into fundamental issues as articulated by a specific perspective. Focusing only on one specific group of likeminded individuals per session, the leader benefits by gaining an understanding of the issues as articulated by the likeminded group. Also, when the focus group technique is used, members benefit from the ability to brainstorm with limited criticism from individuals who have a different viewpoint. Knowing what each perspective believes are the core issues, the leader should invite likeminded participants to work collaboratively to identify ways to overcome the performance inhibitors.

The advantage so far is that by grouping people according to a shared viewpoint, people are likely to explore and communicate without fear of criticism. However, like-mindedness could lead to unproductive groupthink. Thus, the next step is to ask individuals or groups with divergent perspectives to evaluate the intervention ideas generated by the likeminded groups. The group with fresh perspective should be provided background on the perspective to aid in understanding the rationale behind the intervention recommendations. Then the divergent group should be asked to make improvements deemed necessary to ensure the approach is aligned with the needs of both the original and the divergent groups. Finally, the leader must decide whether to implement the consolidated recommendations. Although the process does not guarantee consensus, the recommendations emanating from the five steps to navigating the perspective landscape are more amenable to member needs than if archetypal differences are avoided.

Conclusions

The role of organizations and leaders include formulating strategies to achieve the organization's mission and assuring day-to-day activities are aligned with the organization's short and long-term goals. On the surface, the findings reported in Jones' study (2013) only add to the complexity leaders must navigate. One general belief with three bipolar attitudinal dimensions each with their unique behavioral attributes—seven mechanisms characterizing what organizational members think and do—is daunting. However, the influence of leader behaviors on the perspective landscape and participatory behaviors of organizational members must not be forgotten.

The recommended approach for pursuing an organizational intervention leverages a major presupposition . . . that the leader has the passion for the organization and its mission, compassion for the members, the courage to embark on potentially uncharted territory, and the trustworthiness with organizational members to embark on such a journey. Although Jones (2013) investigated organizational members, the message is intended for leaders and managers.

The five steps address directly the emergence of relationship conflict (Kankanhali et al., 1996), an espoused mediator of process performance effectiveness. Because the five step process involves an ideation process among likeminded individuals followed by an evaluation by individuals with divergent perspectives, the outcomes of the process are likely to have the ownership and buy-in of individuals regardless of perspective. Additionally, according to Cuppen (2010), the evaluation step has self-reinforcing characteristics because the recommendations from each perspective is evaluated for improvement by divergent perspectives. This step could not only be humbling, but also could lead to greater understanding and appreciation for the perspective landscape by process participants.

Last, the five step process provides a framework for managers to implements Senge's (1990) new leadership skills. Although Senge suggested using observational techniques for surfacing and addressing mental models held among members of the organization, the five step process provides a robust method to determine the varied perspectives held given a pre-identified discourse or concourse. The immediate benefit is that subsequent observation in light of understanding the perspective landscape could lead to deeper insight. Admittedly, an almost infinite number of relevant discourses could exist in organizations, observation is more efficient than the recommended five-step process, and it is possible that the inclusive process outlined herein could be difficult to employ in certain sensitive situations. On balance, however, when leaders identify a need for an intervention, the benefits of navigating the perspective landscape outweighs the costs.

Thoughts from the Academic Entrepreneur ™
The problem to be solved:

- Sustainable organizational interventions with higher levels of buy-in

The goals:

- The importance of working relationships and subsequent willingness to participate in the Sales and Operational Planning (S&OP) process.

The questions to ask:

- How can organizations improve the consistency of S&OP implementation results for higher productivity?

Today's Business Application:

- Understand that employees are segmented into four general groups with distinct attitudes, where each group will require a different approach to motivate them.
- Don't be afraid to break your workforce down into small groups, divided by mindset, to better communicate with them.
- Use members of one group to evaluate the ideas of another to prevent destructive groupthink from paralyzing your organization.

References

Cuppen, E. (2010). *Putting perspectives into participation: Constructive conflict methodology for problem structuring in stakeholder dialogues.* Rotterdam, The Netherlands: Uitgeverij BOXPress.

Danielson, S. (2009). Q method and surveys: Three ways to combine Q and R. *Field Methods, 21*(3). 219-237.doi:10.1177/1525822X09332082

Eisenberger, R., Armeli, S., Rexwinkel, B., Lynch, P., & Rhoades, L. (2001). Reciprocation of perceived organizational support. *Journal of Applied Psychology, 86*(1), 42-51. doi:10.1037/0021-9010.86.1.42

Engestrom, Y. (1987). Learning by expanding: An activity theoretical approach to developmental research. Retrieved from http://lchc.ucsd.edu/mca/Paper/Engestrom/expanding/toc.htm

Grimson, J., & Pyke, D. (2007). Sales and operations planning: An exploratory study and framework. *International Journal of Logistics Management, 18*, 322-346. doi:10.1108/09574090710835093

Jones, E. (2013). *Social Exchange Perspective and S&OP Participation.* (Doctoral Dissertation). Available from http://argosy.campusguides.com/eDissertations

Kankanhalli, A., Tan, B., & Wei, K. (2006). Conflict and performance in global virtual teams. *Journal of Management Information Systems, 23*(3), 237-274. doi:10.2753/MIS0742-1222230309

Manz, C., & Sims, H. (1980). Self-management as a substitute for leadership: A social learning theory perspective. *Academy of Management Review, 5*, 361-367. doi:10.5465/AMR.1980.4288845

McKeown, B., & Thomas, D. (1988). *Q Methodology.* Newbury Park, CA: Sage.

Molm, L. (2010). The structure of reciprocity. *Social Psychology Quarterly, 73*(2), 119-131. doi:10.1177/0190272510369079

Palmatier, G., & Crum, C. (2002). *Enterprise sales and operations planning: Synchronizing demand, supply and resources for peak performance.* Boca Raton, FL: J. Ross Publishing.

Senge, P. (1990). The leader's new work: Building learning organizations. *MIT Sloan Management Review, 32*(1), 7-23

Uhl-Bien, M. (1991). *Teamwork of the future: An investigation into teamwork processes of professional work teams in knowledge-based organizations* (Doctoral dissertation). Available from ProQuest Dissertations and Theses (UMI No. 9205408)

Watts, S., & Stenner, P. (2012). *Doing Q methodological research: Theory, method, and interpretation.* London, UK: Sage.

About the Author...

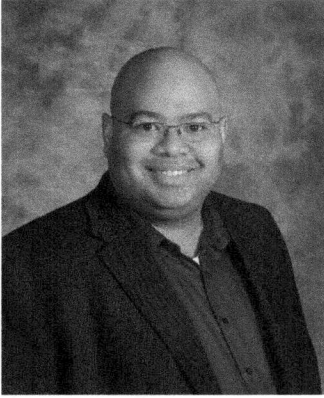

Baltimore native Dr. Ernest Jones holds several accredited degrees: a Bachelor of Science (BS) of Chemical Engineering from Rensselaer Polytechnic Institute, a Master of Business Administration (MBA) with specialization in International Management from Lake Forest Graduate School of Management, and a Doctorate in Business Administration (DBA) with concentration in Management from Argosy University Schaumburg.

Dr. Ernest wrote his research dissertation entitled *Social Exchange Perspective and S&OP Participation,* continues to research organizational behavior topics, and is an author in the award winning series *The Refractive Thinker*®. His research interests include the human factors and dynamics of participatory process effectiveness. He is a scholar-practitioner at heart . . . always seeking to translate theory into practice.

Dr. Ernest is a supply chain professional within the pharmaceutical industry, holds APICS certification in Production and Inventory Management, and is a dedicated student of the theory of constraints. Connect with Dr. Jones through LinkedIn: http://goo.gl/RAoEz.

To reach Dr. Ernest for information on any of these topics, please email:DrErnestJones@gmail.com

CHAPTER 5

Motivation:
Addressing Job-Related Stress and Ensuring Effective
Communication as Best HRM Practices

By Dr. Joseph A. Gioia and Dr. Temeaka Gray

Communication and employee motivation are fundamental components of successful work environments. Effective communication, defined as the formal and informal sharing of timely and meaningful information, influences motivation. Motivation is the act or process that influences others' behavior. In the workplace, the presence of open communication systems and the use of effective communication techniques are likely to motivate employee performance. When motivated, employees may work more effectively toward achieving positive organizational outcomes.

Gioia (2013) and Gray (2013) discussed the constructs of communication and motivation in relation to two studies. Gray (2013) examined the effects of stress and stress management intervention on nurses' motivation, engagement, and retention. Gioia (2013) examined human resource management (HRM) practices used by HRM professionals working in hierarchical organizational cultures to fulfill the needs and expectations of employees and maintain effective constituent relations.

Organizations benefit by motivating employees. Gray (2013) and Gioia (2013) found that effective communication influences the motivation of employees. To apply the findings of these studies to the workplace, the motivation of nurses can be applied to the motivation of most employees in most jobs, whereas the strategies used by HRM professionals can be applied by most managers who must attempt to satisfy the needs and expectations of multiple stakeholders while attempting to motivate and engage employees.

Background Theory

Stress in the Workplace

Most employees experience some degree of stress in their jobs. Stress is a multi-dimensional and open-ended response to the environment (Admi & Mosche-Eilon, 2010; Hobfoll, 1988; Matta, 2010). When stress is constant and left unattended, stress can become a barrier to motivating employees (Hon & Chan, 2013). Because of the challenges of direct patient care and the high demands of their jobs, nurses are at increased risk for experiencing problems associated with work-related stress (Hingley, 1984; Hingley & Cooper, 1986; Hingley & Harris, 1986; Lu, 2008). Nurses routinely complain that a lack of available training to cope with stressors associated with their jobs and their inability to use effective coping mechanisms leads to experiencing increased levels of stress (Gallagher & Gormley, 2009). Stress is a contributor to high nurse turnover and the desire of nurses to leave the nursing profession altogether (Duffield, Roche, & O'Brien-Pallas, 2009; Hodgin, Chandra, & Weaver, 2010; Lu, 2008). The shortage of qualified nurses in the United States is expected to continue to grow with increasing demands for nursing services (Jones, Havens, Thompson, & Knodel, 2008; Lu, 2008). For many organizations, recruitment and retention of qualified nurses will remain a problem (Ambrose, 2002; Van Buskirk, 2001). Of all nurses, managerial nurses have the lowest recruitment and retention rates; a dynamic influenced by job-related stress (Jones et al., 2008).

Self-perceived stress, an individual's view of stress, is responsible for that person's responses to stressors (Cohen, 2006; Matta, 2012). According to Cognitive Activation Theory, workplace demands together with decreased rest and inadequate coping mechanisms can lead to sustained stress activation response (Harris, Ursin, Murison, & Eriksen, 2007). The effects of stress on nurses and self-perceived stress related to nursing roles have been explored (Admi-Moshe-Eilon, 2010; Al-Hussami, 2008; Kashani, Eliasson, Chrosniak, & Vernalis, 2010), although few researchers used a tool aimed at reducing self-perceived stress to compare self-perceived stress in nurses employed in managerial positions to nurses in non-managerial jobs.

Nurses' physical and mental health complaints related to stress have a negative influence on nurses' job performance and individual quality of life (Admi & Mosche-Eilon, 2010; Kashaniet al., 2010; Wong, Wong, Wong, & Lee, 2010). Many organizations implement workplace wellness programs that promote employees' physical, mental, social, and psychological well-being (Merrill, Aldana, Garrett, & Ross, 2011). Successful principles of effective employee wellness programs are based on subjectivity, objectivity, universal truths, and epidemiological research (Schwab & Syme, 1997), but not every employer institutes wellness programs that are effective in mitigating the effects of stress on employees.

Humans are biological, psychological, and social organisms that interact with their environment in positive and negative ways based on individual self-perception of environmental stimuli (Matta, 2012; Roy & Andrews, 1999). According to Selye and

Fortier (1950), some stress is important for motivation and the completion of everyday tasks; however, unrelenting stress can result in complications. These complications, known as distress, can result in negative stress responses having adverse effects on employees' health (Hobfoll, 1988; Matta, 2010; Selye & Fortier, 1950), and possibly becoming employee demotivators. Positive stress responses require adaptation and conscious awareness of stress. With proper training, individuals can manage internal and external stressors in their environment by exercising necessary preventative measures and effective coping mechanisms (Cohen, 2006; Hobfoll, 1988; Roy & Andrews, 1999). Preventing and managing stress enable individuals' adaptation to constant stressors in the environment (Matta, 2012).

The integration of theories of stress, self-perceived stress, and adaptation in the workplace is critical to having a positive influence on the existing nurse shortage, and instrumental in the successful recruitment and retention of qualified nurses. Aside from patient care, nurses should care for their own well-being in the ever-demanding and ever-changing healthcare environment where emphasis on expanding roles places nurses at high risk for burnout (Hingley, 1984; Hingley & Cooper, 1986; Hingley & Harris, 1986). Healthcare organizations should provide stable work environments for their nurses that promote quality care for patients (McHugh, Kutney-Lee, Cimiotti, Sloan, & Aiken, 2011). Two critical elements for employers are to understand the needs of employees, patients, and the organization, and to take effective actions to satisfy those needs (Darling & Heller, 2011; Harter, Schmidt, & Keyes, 2003).

Organizations spend approximately $300 billion annually managing the ineffective organizational dynamics (e.g., absenteeism, decreased motivation, reduced productivity, high employee turnover) associated with employee stress (Cuneo et al.,

2010). Effective stress management and intervention programs can be valuable tools in employee retention (Pipe, Bortz, Dueck, Pendergast, Buchda, & Summers, 2009). Clear communication from employers and opportunities for employees to express self-perceived levels of stress without fear of employer retaliation are critical to the use of programs for managing stress in the workplace (DiFranco, Bressi, & Salzer, 2006; Healey & Marchese, 2006). When given the appropriate resources to prevent or manage stress, employees are more likely to be motivated to perform their jobs well.

Effective Human Resource Management Practices

HRM professionals play an important role in the workplace designing HRM policies, practices, and systems that affect how employees think about and behave in their organizations (Forray, 2006; Simmons, 2008). Many HRM professionals perform tasks associated with personnel management and industrial relations (Boselie, Brewster, & Paauwe, 2009). Personnel management reflects the traditional administrative functions performed by HRM personnel; whereas industrial relations refers to the integrative strategic management functions that contemporary HRM professionals perform. In many organizations, HRM professionals perform the dual roles of HRM, often attempting to balance the conflicting interests of employees and the employer because of each group's differing perceptions and expectations of the HRM function (Boselie et al., 2009). This conflict poses a challenge for HRM professionals who must practice effective HRM (Forray, 2006). As employee retention specialists (Herman, 2005), HRM professionals must satisfy the needs and expectations (i.e., psychological contracts) of line employees (Middlemiss, 2011), while also addressing the multiple competing demands of executives, middle managers, and other organizational stakeholders (Boselie et al., 2009).

Psychological contracts often comprise the entire set of beliefs that employees hold of their organization while engaged in a continual employer-employee exchange relationship (Middlemiss, 2011). When fulfilled, psychological contracts have a positive effect on employee motivation, engagement, job satisfaction, organization commitment, and retention. HRM policies and practices help to shape employees' conscious and unconscious attitudes and beliefs that influence the formation and maintenance of psychological contracts, and may be particularly troublesome when polices and practices are vague or misinterpreted by employees. The terms of psychological contracts are generally implicit and highly subjective, but once formed, psychological contracts strongly influence employees' behavior and can lead to the formation of further and occasionally unreasonable expectations, and cause employees to repeatedly re-evaluate their priorities (Bellou, 2007; Middlemiss, 2011). Any breach of psychological contracts can become serious because of the potential adverse effects on employees' performance (Bull, 2008; Zhao, Wayne, Glibkowski, & Bravo, 2007). HRM professionals play an important role in psychological contract formation and maintenance.

In an open organizational system, the HRM function must interface with a diverse set of individuals, groups, and entities, both internal (e.g., shareholders, executive leadership, middle managers, and employees) and external (e.g., government agencies, professional societies, and the community) to the HRM function. For HRM professionals to be effective in their jobs, they must identify constituents at every level of the organization. As stakeholders, constituents are dependent on, yet exert some degree of control over, the HRM Department (Crow, Hartman, Koen, & Van Epps, 1995; Tsui, 1987). According to Stakeholder

Theory, people working at different levels of an organization may have different needs and expectations, and whether a stakeholder's needs and expectations are satisfied affects individual performance (Freeman, 1984; Graham & Tarbell, 2006).

Many different interacting groups that make competing demands and have very specific and conflicting wants and needs can challenge HRM professionals who attempt to satisfy multiple constituent demands (Crow et al., 1995; Tsui, 1987). Different constituents may be unaware of the critical needs facing the organization, the HRM Department, or the HRM professional, and each constituent group may assume that other constituents are attempting to satisfy their own self-interests (Tsui, 1987). Unawareness and assumptions influence constituents' perceptions of equity within the organization and may result in breach of employees' psychological contracts, which usually has a negative influence on motivation and job performance (Al-Zu'bi, 2010; Crow et al., 1995; Middlemiss, 2011; Saunders & Thornhill, 2003).

Managers must consider the organization's culture as it relates to employees' workplace behavior. Culture is an important consideration for HRM professionals because of culture's far-reaching effects throughout organizations (Jindal, 2011; Simmons, 2008). Hierarchical cultures have a negative influence on employee motivation and job performance because of several dynamics, one being poor communication systems (Jindal, 2011; Simmons, 2008). Of all culture typologies, hierarchical cultures have the most adverse influence on employees' behavior (Cameron & Quinn, 2011). The relationship between culture and performance is reciprocal (Bolman & Deal, 2008; Cameron & Quinn, 2011), and because HRM practices influence both organizational culture and performance, HRM professionals must manage HRM systems that also influence organizational culture and performance.

Characteristics of hierarchical cultures include bureaucracy, formality, a high degree of centralization and standardization, distinct divisions of labor, formal and uniform policies and procedures with strict controls, and a successive chain of command in top-down supervision of leadership (Bolat, Bolat, & Yuksel. 2011; Yu & Wu, 2011). Hierarchical cultures contribute to many problems in organizational effectiveness including impeding open communication throughout the organization; alienating employees; and inhibiting independent decision-making (Bolat et al., 2011; Jindal, 2011). Zeffane, Tipu, and Ryan (2011) found that communication throughout all levels of an organization's hierarchy played a significant role in the relationship between employees' trust and organizational commitment. The perceived effectiveness of the communications between management and organizational agents, such as HRM professionals, and employees were significantly interrelated with employees' trust, organizational commitment, and pride in the organization. Without the presence of clear communication, the relationship between trust and organizational commitment was weak. However, in their research of the literature, Zeffane et al. learned that the leadership style of management and overall organizational culture influence the effectiveness of communication throughout the organization. Some theorists believed that the norm of reciprocity exists with a culture of effective or ineffective communication, each having its own influence on entire organizational culture (Zeffane et al., 2011).

Platonova (2005) found that certain individual cultural characteristics helped organizations sustain a competitive advantage over other organizations, and were associated with high levels of organizational performance. These characteristics included (a) leadership styles of top management; (b) open communication systems; (c) employee empowerment; (d) employee participation in strategic planning and decision-making; and (e) recognition of employees as the source of sustained advantage. These characteristics are found to be strong in various types of organizational culture and are important considerations for most managers. However, the strength of these characteristics is atypical of those found in hierarchical cultures, which are the most traditional of business environments (Jindal, 2011; Yu & Wu, 2011).

Forray (2006) conducted an interpretive research project focusing on the verbal practices of five HRM professionals when engaging others during the creation, application, and interpretation of organizational policies as an alternate approach to examining organizational justice. This approach was non-traditional to studying employees' equity perceptions. Forray introduced the concept of fair organization to organizational justice theory. Fair organization refers to the environment created by HRM professionals to ensure that all organizational members have a common understanding of organizational situations despite the phenomena that individual members bring different orientations and perceptions, and apply different meanings to individual interpretations regardless of the reality of the situation. HRM professionals are instrumental in ensuring the concept of fair organization is transparent in organizations and is an underlying dynamic of communication with constituents.

Methods

Gray (2013) conducted a quantitative study to investigate the relationship between nurses' self-perceived stress and stress management education programs in the workplace. Using a quasi-experimental approach with non-equivalent group design, Gray randomly divided participants into an experimental and a control group unintentionally assigning participants to either group. Nurses employed by acute care agencies, long-term care facilities, and rehabilitation facilities, crossing spectrums of healthcare organizations, participated in the study. Gray informed potential participants that a summary of the study's results would be made available to participants and their organizations, although specific answers and participants' identities would remain confidential. Potential participants completed a demographic questionnaire that Gray used to determine whether participants met the sample criteria for inclusion in the study. Gray used information on the questionnaire to separate participants further into demographic groups for additional data analysis.

Participants consisted of 109 nurses, with varying levels of education, who had worked 16-50 hours per week for at least the previous 12 months. Each participant completed a Cohen's Perceived Stress Scale (PSS); (Cohen, Kamarck, & Mermelstein, 1983) to establish a baseline. Participants in the experimental group were provided with educational materials on stress management, while participants in the control group received no educational materials. To measure the difference in self-perceived stress, participants completed a second PSS at the end of six weeks.

In a qualitative study, Gioia (2013) used a single case research design aligned with case study analysis. Gioia explored the strategies, techniques, and coping mechanisms that HRM professionals working in a managerial role in hierarchical workplace cultures developed to manage the conflict of satisfying the competing demands of internal constituents and maintaining employees' psychological contracts. Eleven HRM professionals who were members of the Long Island (NY) Chapter of the Society for Human Resource Management (SHRM) participated in the study. Participants completed a standard electronic self-report survey questionnaire that included the Organizational Culture

Assessment Instrument (OCAI); (Cameron & Quinn, 2011) to determine participants' culture typology. Participants also responded to 10 open-ended questions focused on participants' experiences and perceptions of their management of the conflict of satisfying the demands of different internal constituent groups and fulfilling employees' psychological contracts. Five of the participants voluntarily participated in a telephonic follow-up interview. Gioia maintained a transcript of each interview.

Gioia (2013) used a coding system to filter, label, and organize data extracted from participants' responses to the questionnaire and interview questions. Coding was necessary for Gioia to identify patterns and themes in participant responses and to further label the data into categories and sub-categories for better interpretation. Categories and sub-categories helped Gioia to identify best HRM practices in consitutent relations.

Participants in Gioia's (2013) study reported their experiences and perceptions of serving and satisfying multiple constituents in their roles as HRM professionals. According to Yap, Holmes, Hannan, and Cukier (2010), HRM professionals would have different experiences and perceptions because the perspectives of members of constituent groups are influenced by their own social cultures, workplace experiences, and many other characteristics. Gioia examined the data for similarities and differences, and discovered more similarities than differences. The presence of more similarities among the data suggested that more managers who serve multiple constituent groups and who work in hierarchical cultures have comparable experiences and use similar practices to satisfy competing demands.

Findings

Stress and Stress Intervention

Gray (2013) found that nurses have a moderately high level of self-perceived stress. Gray did not assess for specific causes of stress, but previous research revealed that nurses reported issues such as self-perceived work/life imbalance, poor communication from employers, and lack of effective stress management training increased levels of self-perceived stress (Cuneo et al., 2010; Gray-Toft & Anderson, 1981). Gray found that nurses employed in managerial positions perceived a greater level of stress than their counterparts working in non-managerial positions. Gray's findings supported previous research (Admi & Moshe-Eilon, 2010) that managerial nurses commonly cite issues such as organizational expectations, limited resources, role conflict, and duty overload as common causes for stress. Gray also found that some employees cited poor communication from management related to employers' possible use of information obtained from the study as a reason not to participate.

Although both participant groups reported a decrease in self-perceived stress, only nurses in the experimental group reported a significant difference. This significant decrease supported Gray's (2013) assumption that nurses provided with educational material designed to assist with stress management would result in a decrease in reported stress levels. Clearly, when employers provide training on preventing and managing stress, employees are more apt to implement effective stress management technique

Cultural Dynamics

Participants in Gioia's (2013) study reported data mostly associated with cultural dynamics prevalent in hierarchical cultures. Gioia organized this data into seven major categories, and further coded and codified data into sub-categories. The seven categories included

    (a) characteristics

    (b) policies and procedures

    (c) communication

    (d) management and leadership

    (e) social behavior

    (f) support for HRM

    (g) challenges for HRM

Data revealed poor vertical (e.g., top-down, bottom-up) communication systems, a lack of organization-wide communication, and poor cross-communication in participants' workplaces. Top-down communication was delayed or distorted, or failed to reach all organizational members as information was filtered down through chains of command. The finding that poor top-down communication was common in hierarchical cultures as information was typically mired within the multiple layers of an organization's reporting structure were consistent with Jindal (2011) and Welch and Welch (2007). Poor top-down communication influenced the integrity of information and impeded bottom-up communication. Gioia (2013) also found inconsistencies in the frequency, timeliness, or quality of formal communication within organizations. These dynamics occasionally caused middle managers and lower level employees to be unaware of executive decisions or the company's goals. In some cases, participants reported that employees felt inhibited by top management, declining to discuss problems or negative situations in the workplace. These feelings failed to motivate or demotivated employees and inhibited bottom-up communication.

Cross-communication was inhibited by a strict adherence to the organization's chain of command or by employees who failed to communicate because they were protective of their own work. Shared knowledge was hindered by an organizational culture that emphasized privacy and confidentiality. In some cases, cross-communication existed but strictly on an as-needed basis when it was essential for employees to share information. In other cases, informal communication existed among long-tenured employees, fostered by their familiarity with each other. Gioia (2013) found that the emphasis on vertical hierarchical structures for communicating information inhibited cross-communication or created barriers to knowledge management processes or activities. Consistent with the literature (Nold, 2012; Tseng, 2010), the conformity of organizational members to uniformity, order, certainty, stability, control, and formality impeded cross-communication. Employees' lack of trust in senior managers further deteriorated communication systems. Consistent with Nold (2012) and Tseng (2010), participants believed that trust in the organization's management was an important cultural element that determined whether employees were comfortable sharing knowledge with others.

Management Strategies and Techniques

Participants in Gioia's (2013) study described how they managed the conflict of satisfying multiple constituent demands and fulfilling employees' psychological contracts. Coding the data, Gioia found patterns and themes that Gioia developed into nine categories, and in some cases, subcategories. Categories included (a) communication; (b) organization skills; (c) education and development; (d) maintaining HRM currency; (e) maintaining organizational currency; (f) customer service; (g) employee appreciation and recognition; (h) recognizing progress; and (i) proaction. Communication, education, and development were relevant dynamics in Gray's (2013) study.

In the category of communication, participants discussed engaging in effective communication. Participants cited that maintaining open communication systems throughout the organization was a good practice referencing such effective strategies as engaging in honest or ongoing communication and ensuring effective communication exists with each constituent group. Gioia (2013) identified two subcategories that included effective communication skills and constituent groups.

Effective communication skills included such activity as actively listening to constituents, having frank discussions with all constituent groups to ensure clearer understanding, and using policies, procedures, or guidelines as a reference to guide discussions. The use of tact and diplomacy when engaged in constituent communication was important for HRM professionals to be effective, especially when communicating with uncivil constituents or dealing with constituents' resistance to change. Maintaining focus on positive discussions and giving positive feedback were good techniques to develop trust and foster good working relationships.

When communicating with different constituent groups, HRM professionals endeavored to understand and respond to the different needs and expectations of each group. A response did not necessarily mean that constituents' needs or expectations were satisfied, but that HRM professionals acknowledged each individual constituent in some way. A very important component of the response strategy was follow-up. Participants engaged in some form of follow-up communication to ensure constituent satisfaction.

By maintaining avenues of open communication and engaging in good communication skills, participants sought to understand and satisfy the different needs and demands of different constituent groups while maintaining employees' psychological contracts and encouraging employee motivation and empowerment. .Participants remained aware that employees' perceptions of the effectiveness of communication between HRM professionals as organizational agents and employees played a significant role in employees' trust and commitment to the organization. By engaging in effective communication skills, HRM professionals established their own expertise with constituents. HRM professionals also provided employees with the opportunities to be heard, often when employees had no opportunities to communicate upward or outward. These practices were consistent with Forray's (2006) concept of fair organization.

Education and Development

Participants in Gioia's (2013) study discussed education and development as those activities aimed to maintain effective relationships among constituents throughout the organization. Participants used a variety of formal and informal education and training strategies to develop constituents and maintain good constituent relations. Education and development took place in a variety of settings (e.g., classroom, online, private one-on-one) or was delivered by a variety of modalities (e.g., on-site instructor, E-learning, self-instruct workbooks, open discussions). Training was usually specific to the needs of different constituent groups. Participants focused on effective methods to develop employees' competencies, knowledge, skills, and abilities, and build effective relationships. Participants reported that education and development activities helped them to forge effective relationships with different constituent groups. These activities also served to enhance HRM professionals' credibility and expertise and reduce incidences of counterproductive workplace behavior. These findings were consistent with the findings of Bowen and Ostroff (2004) and Simmons (2008). By educating employees about organizational situations including the reasons for business decisions or the business necessity to satisfy the needs or expectations of one constituent group over another, HRM professionals worked towards influencing constituents' perceptions of equity in the organization. These efforts supported the findings of several researchers (Al-Zu'bi, 2010; Crow et al., 1995; Saunders & Thornhill, 2003).

The effect of stress management education was critical to the nurses in the experimental group in Gray's (2013) study. By helping those participants to better manage the job-related stressors that challenge nurses, there was a significant decrease in their self-perceived level of stress. Leaders and managers should evaluate the training and development needs in their organizations and align themselves with HRM professionals, when possible, to ensure that employees receive the necessary education to acquire or develop the essential competencies and skill sets to effectively perform their jobs.

Conclusion

Effective communication has a strong influence on motivating employees in an organization. Employers that share meaningful information vertically and horizontally across disciplines are likely to create good working environments and facilitate good working relationships between managers and employees. The use of clear concise communication methods when integrated with open communication systems helps managers to facilitate sufficient and effective exchanges of information. Having access to complete information can be a valuable resource that helps motivate employees to perform their jobs.

HRM professionals are instrumental in encouraging fair and ethical work practices within organizations. Generally, HRM professionals have a high degree of influence satisfying the needs of people, departments, and entire organizations. This level of influence places burden on HRM professionals to ensure open lines of communication and motivational activities exist in the workplace. However, managers throughout an organization should share the responsibility of managing these activities.

Gray (2013) concluded that nurses experience a moderately high level of self-perceived stress. Poor communication within their organizations was a cause of increased stress among nurses. Although communication was not a variable in Gray's study, communication did play a very important role. Regardless of whether Gray or the employer-organization directed the study, the option to participate remained in the control of employees. Receiving phone calls from potential participants, Gray became aware that nurses who did not trust their organizations were unwilling to participate in the study. Potential participants cited lack of communication on the part of their employers as a reason not to participate in the study.

Gioia (2013) concluded that the strategies used by participants in the study were consistent with best practices used by HRM professionals in various work settings. HRM professionals in Gioia's study did not develop and implement strategies that were unique to the dynamics of hierarchical culture. Given that hierarchical culture is the most restrictive of culture typologies and the culture that least motivates employees, the best practices identified in Gioia's study may be used in most workplaces. These best HRM practices are effective business practices for most managers when communicating with and motivating employees.

Employers should understand the demands of employees' jobs. Employers may find that their organizations operate more effectively when managers apply communication practices that help employees to understand the needs and desires of the organization, and to perform their jobs well. In addition, employers should identify the workplace stressors that may adversely affect employees' motivation. Managers should attempt to mitigate stressors and provide education in stress prevention and management to help engage employees. When employees have complete information and are able to function with manageable levels of stress, they are more likely to be motivated and productive.

Thoughts from the Academic Entrepreneur™

The problem to be solved:

- Lack of effectively motivated employees to work toward achieving positive organizational outcomes because of poor recruitment and retention strategies

The goals:

- To apply best practices in motivation in the fields of Nursing and HRM Professionals, to satisfy the needs and expectations of multiple stakeholders while attempting to motivate and engage employees.

The questions to ask:

- How can one recruit and retain qualified personnel regarding the stress of the workplace regarding employee shortages?

Today's Business Application

- This may seem like a no-brainer, but don't neglect stress management training for employees in inherently high-stress positions.
- When a job is stressful, management can help by eliminating as many other sources of workplace stress as possible. Transparency in (and good communication about) executive decisions is an important part.

- Allow and encourage lateral communication within the team, so that everyone has a chance to be heard.

References

Admi, H., & Moshe-Eilon, Y. (2010). Stress among charge nurses: Tool development and stress measurement. *Nursing Economics, 28*(3), 151-158. Retrieved from http://www.ncbi.nlm.gov/pubmed/20672537

Al-Hussami, M. (2008). A study of nurses' job satisfaction: The relationship to organizational commitment, perceived organizational support, transactional leadership, transformational leadership, and level of education. *European Journal of Scientific Research, 22*(2), 286-295. Retrieved from http://www.eurojournals.com/ejsr.htm

Al-Zu'bi, H. A. (2010). A study of relationship between organizational justice and job satisfaction. *International Journal of Business and Management, 5*(12), 102-109. Retrieved from http://www.ccsenet.org/journal/index.php/ijbm/article/view/8495/6335

Ambrose, C. (2002). Recruitment problems in intensive care: A solution. *Nursing Standard, 17*(12), 39-40.Retrieved from http://www.nursing-standard-journal.co.uk

Bellou, V. (2007). Shaping psychological contracts in the public and private sectors: A human resources management perspective. *International Public Management Journal, 10*, 327-349. doi:10.1080/10967490701515515

Bolat, T., Bolat, O. I., & Yuksel, M. (2011). Relationship between role ambiguity and burnout: The meditative effect of organizational culture. *Interdisciplinary Journal of Contemporary Research in Business, 2*, 373-398. Retrieved from http://ijcrb.webs.com/archives.htm

Bolman, L. G., & Deal, T. E. (2008). Reframing organizations: Artistry, choice, and leadership (4th ed.). San Francisco, CA: Jossey-Bass.

Boselie, P., Brewster, C., & Paauwe, J. (2009). In search of balance – Managing the dualities of HRM: An overview of the issues. *Personnel Review, 38*, 461-471. doi:10.1108/00483480910977992

Bowen, D., & Ostroff, C. (2004). Understanding HRM-firm performance linkages: The role of the "strength" of the HRM system. *Academy of Management Review, 29*(2), 203-221. doi:10.5465/AMR.2004.12736076

Bull, R. A. (2008). *Psychological contract under-fulfillment: Leader-member crossover* (Doctoral dissertation). Retrieved from ProQuest Dissertations and Theses database. (UMI No. 3342408)

Cameron, K. S., & Quinn, R. E. (2011). Diagnosing and changing organizational culture: Based on the competing values framework (3rd ed.). San Francisco, CA: Jossey-Bass.

Cohen, J. (2006). The aging nursing workforce: How to retain experienced nurses. *Journal of Healthcare Management, 51*(4), 233-245. doi:10.1037/0278-6133.9.4.466

Cohen, S., Kamarck, T., & Mermelstein, R. (1983). A global measure of perceived stress. *Journal of Health and Social Behavior, 24*, 386-396. Retrieved from http://www.asanet.org/journals/jhsb/jhsb.cfm#articles

Crow, S., Hartman, S., Koen, C., & Van Epps, P. (1995). A constituency theory perspective of human resources effectiveness. *Employee Relations, 17*(1), 38-50. doi:10.1108/01425459510078360

Cuneo, C., Cooper, M., Drew, C., Naoum-Heffernan, C., Sherman, T., Walz, K., & Weinberg, J. (2010). The effects of reiki on work-related stress of the registered nurse. *Journal of Holistic Nursing, 29*(1), 33-43. doi:10.1177/0898010110377294

Darling, J., & Heller, V. (2011). The key for effective stress management: Importance of responsive leadership in organizational development. *Organizational Development Journal, 29*(1), 9-26.

DiFranco, E., Bressi, S., & Salzer, M. (2006). Understanding consumer preferences for communication channels to create consumer-directed health promotion efforts in psychiatric rehabilitation settings. *Psychiatric Rehabilitation Journal, 29*(4), 251-257. doi:10.2975/29.2006.251.257

Duffield, C., Roche, M., O'Brien-Pallas, L., & Catling-Paull, C. (2009). The implications of staff 'churn' for nurse managers, staff, and patients. *Nursing Economics, 27*(2), 103-110. Retrieved from http://www.nursingeconomics.net

Forray, J. M. (2006). Sustaining fair organization: An interpretive view of justice in organizational life. *Group & Organization Management, 31*, 359-387. doi:10.1177/1059601105275658

Freeman, R. E. (1984). *Strategic management: A stakeholder approach.* Boston, MA: Pitman.

Gallagher, R., & Gormley, D. K. (2009). Perceptions of stress, burnout, and support systems in pediatric bone marrow transplantation nursing. *Clinical Journal of Oncology Nursing, 13*, 681–685. doi:10.1188/09.

SJON.681-68

Gioia, J. A. (2013). *HRM professionals' management of constituents' demands and psychological contracts in hierarchical cultures* (Doctoral dissertation). Retrieved from ProQuest Dissertations and Theses database. (UMI No. 3590283)

Graham, M. E., & Tarbell, L. M. (2006). The importance of the employee perspective in the competency development of human resource professionals. *Human Resource Management, 45,* 337-355. doi:10.1002/hrm.20116

Gray, T. (2013). *Exploring self-perceived stress and stress management in managerial and non-managerial nurses* (Doctoral dissertation). Retrieved from ProQuest Dissertations and Theses database. (UMI No. 3566486)

Gray-Toft, P., & Anderson, T. G. (1981). Stress among hospital nursing staff: Its causes and effects. *Social Science and Medicine, 15A,* 539-647.

Harris, A., Ursin, H., Murison, R., & Eriksen, H. (2007). Coffee, stress and cortisol in nursing staff. *Psychoneuroendocrinology, 32,* 332-330. doi:10.1016/j.psyneun.207.01.003

Harter, J., Schmidt, F., & Keyes, C. (2003). Well-being in the workplace and its relationships to business outcomes. In C. L. M. Keyes & J. Haidt (Eds.), *Flourishing: the positive person and the good life* (pp. 205-244). Washington, DC: American Psychological Association. Retrieved from http://media.gallup.com/DOCUMENTS/whitePaper--Well-BeingInTheWorkplace.pdf

Healey, B., & Marchese, M. (2006). The use of marketing tools to increase participation in worksite wellness programs. *Academy of Health Care Management Journal, 2,* 75-83. Retrieved from http://www.alliedacademies.org/Public/Journals

Herman, R. E. (2005). HR managers as employee-retention specialists. *Employee Relations Today, 32*(2), 1-7. doi:10.1002/ert.20058

Hingley, P. (1984). The humane face of nursing. *Nursing Mirror, 159,* 19-22.

Hingley, P., & Cooper, C. L. (1986). *Stress and the nurse manager.* Chichester, UK: John Wiley.

Hingley, P., & Harris, P. (1986). Burnout at the senior level. *Nursing Times, 30,* 28-29. Retrieved from http://www.nursingtimes.net

Hobfoll, S. (1988). *The ecology of stress*. PA: Hemisphere.

Hodgin, R. F., Chandra, A., & Weaver, C. (2010). Correlates to long-term-care nurse turnover: Survey results from the state of West Virginia. *Hospital Topics, 88*(4), 91-96. doi:10.1080/00185868.2010.528258

Hon, A., & Chan, W. (2013). The effects of group conflict and work stress on employee performance. *Cornell Hospitality Quarterly, 54*(2), 174-184. Retrieved from http://www.hotelschool.cornell.edu/about/pubs/publications/quarterly/

Jindal, R. (2011). Reducing the size of internal hierarchy: The case of multi-unit franchising. *Journal of Retailing, 87*, 549-562. doi:10.1016/jretai.2011.07.003

Jones, C., Havens, D., Thompson, P., & Knodel, L. (2008). Chief nursing officer retention and turnover: A crisis brewing? Results of a national survey. *Journal of Healthcare Management, 53*(2), 89-106. Retrieved form http://www.ache.org/pubs/jhm/jhm_index.cfm

Kashani, M., Eliasson, A., Chrosniak, L., & Vernalis, M. (2010). Taking aim at nurse stress: A call to action. *Military Medicine, 175*(2), 96-100. Retrieved from http://www.amsus.org/index.php/journal

Lu, J. L. (2008). Organizational role stress indices affecting burnout among nurses. *Journal of International Women's Studies, 9*(3), 63-78. Retrieved from http://vc.bridgew.edu/jiws/

Matta, C. (2012). *The stress response*. Oakland, CA: New Harbinger Publications.

McHugh, M., & Brennan, S. (1993). Managing work stress: A key issue for all organization members. *Employee Counseling Today, 5*(1), 16. Retrieved from http://www.emeraldinsight.com/journals.htm?issn=0955-8217

Merrill, R. M., Aldana, S. G., Garrett, J., & Ross, C. (2011). Effectiveness of a workplace wellness program for maintaining health and promoting healthy behaviors. *Journal of Occupational and Environmental Medicine, 53*, 782-787. Retrieved from http://journals.lww.com/joem/pages/default.aspx

Middlemiss, S. (2011). The psychological contract and implied contractual terms: Synchronous or asynchronous models? *International Journal of Law and Management, 53*(1), 32-50. doi:10.1108/17542431111111872

Nold III, H. A. (2012), Linking knowledge processes with firm performance: Organizational culture. *Journal of Intellectual Capital, 13*(1), 16-38. doi:10.1108/14691931211196196

Platonova, E. A. (2005). *The relationship among human resource management, organizational culture, and organizational performance* (Doctoral dissertation). Retrieved from ProQuest Dissertations and Theses database. (UMI No. 3201176)

Pipe, T., Bortz, J., Dueck, A., Pendergast, D., Buchda, V., & Summers, J. (2009). Nurse leader mindfulness meditation program for stress management: A randomized controlled trial. *Journal of Nursing Administration, 39*(3), 130-137. doi:10.1097/NNA.06013e31819894a0

Roy, C., & Andrews, H. A. (1999). *The Roy adaptation model* (2nd ed.). Stanford, CT: Appleton & Lange.

Saunders, M. N. K., & Thornhill, A. (2003). Organisational justice, trust and the management of change: An exploration. *Personnel Review, 32*, 360-375. doi:10.1108/00483480310467660

Schwab, M., & Syme, S. (1997). On paradigms, community participation, and future of public health. *American Journal of Public Health, 87*, 2049-2050. doi:10.2105/AJPH.87.12.2049

Selye, H., & Fortier, C. (1950). Adaptive reaction to stress. *Psychosomatic Medicine, 12*(3), 149-157. Retrieved from http://www.psychosomaticmedicine.org/

Simmons, D. C. (2008). *Organizational culture, workplace incivility, and turnover: The impact of human resources practices* (Doctoral dissertation). Retrieved from ProQuest Dissertations and Theses database. (UMI No. 3308361)

Tseng, S. (2011). The effects of hierarchical culture on knowledge management processes. *Management Research Review, 33*, 827-839. doi:10.1108/01409171011065635

Tsui, A. S. (1987). Defining the activities and effectiveness of the human resources department: A multiple constituency approach. *Human Resource Management, 26*(1), 35-69. doi:10.1002.hrm.3930260104

Van Buskirk, S. (2001). The nursing shortage: take it personal. *Nephrology Nursing Journal, 28,* 368. Retrieved from http://www.annanurse.org/nnj

Welch, J., & Welch, S. (2007, June 25). Lay off the layers. *Business Week*, 96. Retrieved from http://www.businessweek.com/

Wong, H., Wong, M., Wong, S., & Lee, A. (2010). The association between shift duty and abnormal eating behavior among nurses working in a major hospital: A cross-sectional study. *International Journal of Nursing, 47*(8), 1021. doi:10.1016/j.jnurstu.2010.01.001

Yap, M., Holmes, M. R., Hannan, C., & Cukier, W. (2010). The relationship between diversity training, organizational commitment, and career satisfaction. *Journal of European Industrial Training, 34*, 519-538. doi:10.1108/03090591011061202

Yu, T., & Wu, N. (2011). Bureaucratic hierarchy vs. feudal hierarchy: A study on the organization culture of China's SOEs. *International Journal of Business and Management, 6*(2), 139-146. Retrieved from http://www.ccsenet.org/journal/index.php/ijbm/article/view/9180/6723

Zeffane, R., Tipu, S. A., & Ryan, J. C. (2011). Communication, commitment & trust: Exploring the triad.

International Journal of Business and Management, 6(6), 77-87. Retrieved from http://www.ccsenet.org/journal/index.php/ijbm/article/view/10815/7672

Zhao, H., Wayne, S. J., Glibkowski, B. C., & Bravo, J. (2007). The impact of psychological contract breach on

work-related outcomes: A meta-analysis. *Personnel Psychology, 60*, 647-681. doi:10.1111/j.1744-6570.2007.00087.x

About the Author...

Residing in Wayne, NJ, Dr. Joseph A. Gioia holds several accredited degrees; a Bachelor of Arts (BA) in Special Education from William Paterson University; a Master of Science (MS) in Human Resources Management from The New School; and a Doctor of Psychology (PsyD) in Business Psychology from the University of the Rockies. His doctoral dissertation, *HRM Professionals' Management of Constituents' Demands and Psychological Contracts in Hierarchical Cultures,* was recognized with the Distinguished Doctoral Dissertation Scholarship. He is a member of The Golden Key International Honour Society.

Dr. Joe holds a post-graduate certificate in Organization Development also from The New School. He is a Certified Employee Benefits Specialist (CEBS) and a Compensation Management Specialist (CMS).

Dr. Joe held several high level positions in human resources management (HRM) in both the for-profit and non-profit sectors. He is currently a business psychologist and consultant in organizational leadership, organization development, change management, HRM, employee benefits, and compensation management. Dr. Joe is a member of the Society for Human Resource Management (SHRM) and the International Society of Certified Employee Benefits Specialists (ISCEBS). He serves on the faculty of Ashford University and Touro University Worldwide, teaching courses in business, management, and organizational psychology.

To reach Dr. Joe for information on consulting or doctoral coaching, please email: jagpsyd@outlook.com

About the Author...

Dr. Temeaka Gray resides in the midwestern town of Toledo, Ohio. Dr. Temeaka holds several accredited degrees; a Master of Business Administration (MBA) from Tiffin University; a Master of Nursing (MSN) from the University of Cincinnati; and a Doctorate in Psychology (Health and Wellness focus) from the University of the Rockies.

Dr. Temeaka, an Assistant Professor at The University of Toledo, teaches and works with students across undergraduate, graduate, and doctoral curriculums in the nursing program. She enjoys teaching and mentoring in psychological, sociological, and nursing disciplines. She is a member of the American Psychological Association, the Ohio Association of Advanced Practice Nurses, Sigma Theta Tau International, and Delta Sigma Theta Sorority, Inc.

Dr. Temeaka is a Certified Nurse Practitioner at A Woman's Answer and owns Epiphany Health Services. She is the Vice Chairperson of the Diversity Committee at the University of Toledo College of Nursing. Her doctoral study, *Exploring Stress and Stress Management in Managerial and Non-managerial Nurses*, afforded her the chance to gain professional and academic expertise to facilitate understanding within the healthcare community.

To reach Dr. Temeaka for information on consulting or doctoral coaching, please email: temeaka.gray@gmail.com

CHAPTER 6

*Using Qualitative Methods to
Discover Reasons for Leaders' Failure*

By Dr. Annie Brown

The topic of leadership continues to be highly debated. Diverse interpretations exist concerning what constitutes a clearly defined leader. Individuals have differing opinions concerning the qualities of a successful leader versus those of an unsuccessful leader. As McCuddy and Cavin (2008) contended, numerous factors affect the effectiveness of a leader. Leadership effectiveness is dependent primarily on leaders' success based on the completion of a set of goals within an established timeline (McCuddy & Cavin, 2008). Leaders are expected to cause certain events (Burns, 2010) in a timely manner. People will focus attention on those events and will derive a perception based on the results. In this exploratory study, I investigated some of the perceptions in an attempt to determine the reasons some leaders such as educational leaders are unsuccessful in their quest to lead others when attempting to respond to organizational goals.

The approach I took to study leadership may not be a popular approach. I chose not to use a *business as usual* approach, such as studying reasons leaders are effective, to discover facts about leadership. Instead, Brown (2005) study focused on leadership failure. Solutions to leadership problems will help propel more leaders to success, and organizational effectiveness will improve because of pertinent facts discovered by using a qualitative grounded theory method. More intense debates about leadership may occur as a result of what I discovered.

Overview of the Study

Leadership problems are societal problems. Millions of dollars are spent training leaders to be effective. Yet, leaders are still failing to be effective thus negatively impacting organizations (Gentry & Sparks, 2012). Effective leaders are expected to guide their organization to success (Bennis, 2013; Green & Cooper (2012; 2013); Sakiru, D'Silva, Othman, DaudSilong, & Busayo, 2013). A Booz Allen study revealed that 80% of businesses fail (Shenkman, 2004). Many of the organizations could attribute their substandard performance to poor leadership and leadership turnover. Concerns have escalated about leadership turnover in educational organizations such as community colleges (Katsinas, D'Amico, & Friedel, 2012). The reasons for the leaders' departures are numerous. Yet, as Ready and Conger (2008) indicated finding and retaining good talent is difficult. Consequently, as research indicated, a significant number of organizations classify their leaders as failures (Bennis, 1997; Kaiser, Hogan, & Craig, 2008; Shenkman, 2004). Unsurprisingly, educational leaders are not exempt from failure because some of them also fail to complete assigned tasks. A gap exists in the literature because only a small amount of scholarly publications directly reveal information on the failure of leaders and, more specifically, educational leaders in comparisons to published peer reviewed scholarly communication about leadership effectiveness (Brown, 2005).

When leaders fail, especially educational leaders, negative

impacts occur on society because education is a critical component of society. Because of the importance of education, the failures of educational leaders have significant social influence. Hence, a need to know and understand why educational leaders fail exists. Leading an organization effectively is challenging, yet essential (Spears & Parker, 2013). Educational leaders who are effective benefit the organization and the public (Katsinas et al, 2012).

The Brown (2005) research study offers an understanding of reasons some educational leaders fail to complete their assigned tasks. Themes inherent in unsuccessful leaders in an educational setting are revealed. The information gathered and the inherent themes will serve as a basis for further studies in diverse organizations. Hopefully, organizational leaders will apply the lessons learned to leadership in an effective manner. Furthermore, communicating more information on reasons leaders fail will serve as a catalyst to significantly increase the effectiveness of some organizations (Armstrong, 2009).

Background and Theory

Leaders who succeed and leaders who fail affect an organization, the former positively and the later negatively, knowing reasons leaders are successful and why the leaders are unsuccessful is critical. Oftentimes, detrimental problems that organizations experience can be attributed to disparate leadership (Brown, 2005). Some organizations classify a leader as a failure, but the reasons for doing so could be unclear (Brown, 2005).

The abundant literature theories, rules, strategies, and biographies of successful leaders are published in textbooks, peer-reviewed journals, and other online publications (e.g. Bass, 1990; Bennis, 2013; Bennis & Nanus, 1985; Fiedler, 1971; Kotter, 1990; Yukl, 2006; Zaccaro, 2007). In contrast, a comprehensive examination of the literature indicates less research conducted on leadership failure (Brown, 2005). A search of peer reviewed articles revealed literature about why leaders fail is often imbedded in other topics on leadership (i.e., leaders and followers, effective leadership, attributes of a good leader, and leadership in the new paradigm) which made obtaining specific information on the reasons leaders are unsuccessful difficult (Brown, 2005).

Most of the literature on leadership supports the contention that leaders have a tremendous influence on the behaviors, attitudes, and performance of their subordinates (Yukl, 2012). Hence, leaders must have a relationship with their subordinates (Brill & Sloan, 2011). Vidyarthi, Erdogan, Anand, & Liden (2014) and Birnbaum (1992) communicated that there must be a *leader* and *led* relationship. In other words, there must be an individual or a group of individuals to lead, and there must be an individual or group to take the lead. This leader-led relationship could be of a formal nature such as an organization's president or Chief Executive Officer (CEO) or informal in which no formal structure exists. Regardless of whether it is a formal or informal leader, leader turnover is destabilizing and has the potential to increase employee turnover at every level of the organization (Dulebohn, Bommer, Liden, Brouer, & Ferris, 2012; Downey, 2001). However, Brown (2005) research focused on formal leadership positions.

When an organization has to replace a leader a ripple effect occurs throughout the organization (Downey, 2001; Dulebohn et al., 2012). A high correlation between job satisfaction and the relationship between the employee and direct supervisors and managers exist (Downey, 2001; Sakiru et al., 2013). At times, employees leave the organization because of the leader's substandard performance or departure from the organization (Brown, 2005)

The leader is not the only person with the option to leave the organization because of the inability to lead effectively. The leader's exit and or the employees' departure have the potential to weaken customer relationships in an organization. Strategic advantages result when the organization determines accurately why the leader failed to satisfy the supervisory needs of the organization. A robotic approach or *business as usual* approach to discovering the reason(s) a leader failed is counter-productive (Sallie & Flood, 2012).

Leaders exit organizations for multiple reasons. When the leaders depart, others could deem the leader a failure (Brown, 2005). Recognizing the possible negative effects on the organization, many organizations are pro-active in trying to avoid sub-standard performance in leaders. The organizations attempt to ensure leaders are successful. So, organizations conduct workshops on effective leadership. Brill and Sloan (2011) explained that effective leadership continues to be a primary concern of organizations.

Despite of the leadership workshops conducted and the critical role of the leader, leaders still exit organizations for various negative reasons. In many instances, organizations give vague reasons for the leaders' departure. Frequently, organizations disclose little or no substantive information to employees or to others external to the organization why the leaders depart. Yet, the reasons leaders fail are generally known, and employees of the organizations could be aware of many of the reasons. Still, the employees are reluctant to share the reasons (Brown, 2005).

In researching an expanded database of leadership literature, Brown (2005) discovered an abundance of publications on leadership success, leadership effectiveness, or leadership in general while in comparison only a limited number of peer-reviewed publications on leadership failure. The organization could seize an opportunity to correct leadership disparities and increase the potential to improve the organization's effectiveness when employers or leaders share and communicate reasons for leadership failure. Feedback from employees about leaders could be one of the most important aspects of any organization. Employers could use the information collected to take corrective actions that would significantly improve the effectiveness of the organization. The focus of Brown (2005) study was to gain sound evidence regarding why some senior level educational leaders who have the authority and responsibility for an organization are not successful at completing assigned task.

Literature Review

The formal study of leadership is still an elusive phenomenon (Shushok & Moore, 2010). Leadership is the most essential component of an organization (Gentry, 2012). As would be expected, the definitions of leadership are innumerable. Vast numbers of leadership theories (Beyer, 2012; Fiedler, 1971) exist. Leadership gurus agree that leadership is a critical element of any organization (Bennis, 2013; Yukl, 2012)

Leadership gives one person power over another (Fieldler 1971 as cited in Kalaluhi, 2013; Fiedler, 1971). With such power, men have the capability to accomplish things that would be nearly impossible to do independently (Fieldler 1971 as cited in Kalaluhi, 2013; Fiedler, 1971). In 1996, leadership guru Peter Drucker compared leadership to a computer composed of complex and simple components (Drucker, 1996). Comprehending the intricacies of a computer is difficult; so is it with understanding leadership. Admittedly, leadership and its components cannot be defined with precision.

In one acceptable definition of leadership, a leader is defined as a person who has the authority to decide, direct, and fulfill the objectives of an organization (Portnoy, 1986; Tost, Gino,

& Larrick, 2011). True leaders have a clear vision and can get others to share in it (Bennis, 1989; DePree, 1989; Drucker, 1996; Griffin, Parker, & Mason, 2010). Many debates occur about who meets the qualifications to be a true leader. After reviewing diverse number of leadership theories Brown (2005) deduced a great deal of misunderstanding exists about what it means to be a bona fide leader. Yet, the definitions of leadership are substantive when explaining who leaders are and what leaders do. Undoubtedly, some leaders are more able to be successful to lead than other leaders.

The question what makes a person a leader is posed? The evidence proves the question is by no means original. In 1787, when the Founding Fathers were in Philadelphia creating the U. S. Constitution, questions surfaced about leaders' role. As questions surfaced about the role of political leaders, concerns about leadership and leaders were evident (Brill & Sloan, 2011). As the literature reveals, even though there have been enormous amounts of research on leadership since the days of the Founding Fathers, scholars have not reached consensus on the definition of a leader (Brown, 2005). Likewise, inconsistency prevails in the countless responses to the question *what makes a successful leader?*

As changes occur in facets of the world, the leadership challenges increase. Bennis (2013; 1997) surmised that global challenges and changes of the millennium mandate new forms of leadership. The new generation of corporate leaders must know the importance of developing through the ages (Bennis, 2013; Bennis, 1997; Brown, 2011). Of particular concern is leadership in the educational system. According to the League for Innovation in the Community College (Abts, 2013), community colleges are phenomenal success stories in the U. S. higher education system. Yet, concerns about the state of leadership in community colleges have increased (Amey & VanDerlinden, 2002; Cohen &

Brawer, 2008; Katsinas et al., 2012; Little, 2002; Shults, 2001; Wolf & Carroll, 2002). Valid reason exists for concerns because community college leaders play a major role in their communities and in economic and workplace development. Community colleges enroll diverse groups of learners including young adults who enroll after graduating from high school. Community colleges have a continuing responsibility to society to develop contributing citizens to society (Brown, 2005; Katsinas et al., 2012). The college leaders are visible, but their turnover rate is increasing (Edddy, 2013; Katsinas et al., 2012). Some of the reasons are known, but others are not.

Many leaders stand at the crossroad between success and failure. The action(s) the leaders take can be a determining factor in what the leaders become. If leaders take actions necessary to ensure their success, the leaders will not fail. However, leaders who fail could never learn what to do to become effective leaders. If the leader fails, organizations are affected adversely. Leaders who do not perform actions that move the organization forward -- do not focus on the needs of the organization or who do not satisfy the organization's mission are deemed failures. College presidents who fail lose the support of faculty, administrators, and trustees (Birnbaum, 1992; Vidyarthi et al., 2014). Leadership problems extend to all types of organizations. Failure is one of the paths college presidents take -- with the other two being modal and exemplary (Birnbaum, 1992; Vidyarthi et al., 2014).

Little doubt, organizational leaders determine the success or failure of an organization (Beyer, 2012; Gentry, 2012; Fiedler, 1971). Behaviors regarded as critical incidents distinguish successful leaders from failed leaders. The goal of Brown (2005) study was to discover those behaviors in failed leaders.

Data Analysis Research Method and Design

The art of discovery is a monumental task. Many strategies could be used. A strategy that yields grounded theory is effective for making predictions and explaining behavior (Sallee & Flood, 2012). Qualitative grounded theory research methodology is an effective method to use to discover more information (Gordon, 2011; Sallee & Flood, 2012) about leadership failure (Brown, 2005). Qualitative researchers want to discover new information or new ways of doing things (Sallee & Flood, 2012). Qualitative research covers several forms of inquiry that help individuals understand and explain the meaning of social phenomena (Gordon, 2011; Merriam, 2001). One of the main goals of Brown (2005) qualitative grounded theory study was to identify factors inherent in unsuccessful leaders. The information gathered and inherent themes will serve as a basis for further studies in diverse organizations, and organizational leaders could apply the lessons learned to leadership in an effective manner.

The target population for this study included senior and middle level leaders from a community college system, each possessing more than 10 years of leadership experience in the community college educational environment. The demographics of the participants in the survey are diverse with 15 males and 12 females from different geographical regions (Brown, 2005). The participants interact with senior-level leaders at least weekly. With Brown's (2005) use of semi-structured interviews, the leaders shared their perspectives of leadership failures in education by responding to questions from the researcher's self-designed leadership questionnaire surrounding the seven following research questions:

1. What makes a leader successful?
2. What constitutes leader failure?
3. Why did the leader fail?

4. What leadership style did the leader utilize?
5. What were the failed leader's strengths and weaknesses?
6. How did the leader's failure affect the organization?
7. What lessons were learned from the leader's failure?

As the researcher, my astuteness and extensive knowledge of the interview process and excellent interpersonal skills contributed to my being able to obtain valid and reliable data in an ethical manner. With the use of Nud*ist, a qualitative software program, and the word processor, I analyzed the data in a manner that produced themes.

Findings
One goal of the study was to identify factors inherent in unsuccessful leaders. The information gathered and any inherent themes will serve as a basis for further studies in diverse organizations. Leaders of organizations could apply the lessons learned in an effective manner.

Overwhelmingly, the participants in the study stated the lack of leadership skills and ineffective communication are two of the main reasons leaders fail to complete their assigned tasks. Other interesting and unique reasons surfaced. Communication problems included the leader's failure to communicate organizational goals and changes, the leader's failure to listen to others' opinions, and the leader's inability to talk to employees of the organization. The themes that emerged from the responses to the questions are reported here. The supporting statements from the participants will not be included because of their magnitude and specificity.

I ascertained that the participants could identify attributes of successful leaders prior to questioning the participants about leadership failure. The participants' responses about what makes a leader successful included sixteen attributes including the ability to communicate effectively, teamwork, visionary, love of job, sincerity, knowledge of job, the ability to make tough decisions, and the ability to get along with others. The major themes about leadership failure are listed in Table 1. Ninety-three percent (25 of 27) had firsthand knowledge of leaders who failed to fulfill their job duties in the community college system and were terminated, demoted or resigned. Seven percent (2 of 27) did not have firsthand knowledge but shared their perspectives about leaders and leadership failure in the community college system. Included in Table 1 are participants' perceptions of the failed leaders' leadership style and major weaknesses.

Leadership Failure Themes

Reasons leaders fail (in general): Inability to communicate; lack of support, insensitivity; divisive; lack of knowledge; close-minded; lack of integrity; lack of sincerity; selfish; lack of vision; fails to motivate; and does not get along with others.

Most prevalent reasons leaders fail (firsthand knowledge): Lack of communication; lack of leadership skills; lack of commitment; lack of trust; cultural differences; and lack of fairness.

Least prevalent reasons leaders fail (firsthand knowledge): Paranoid; not a team player; refusal to delegate; lack of integrity; vision disparity; lack of respect; selfish; dishonesty; and unfair.

Perceived leadership style of failed leaders: Authoritarian; authoritarian and somewhat laissez-faire; autocratic; people oriented; and no leadership style.

Perceived major weaknesses of failed leaders: Lack of knowledge; unprofessional; autocratic; failure to understand political environment; failure to build spirit of teamwork; inability to use technology; excessive non-work related conversations; refused to see signs of demise; and poor interpersonal skills.

Participants' identity remains anonymous. One participant said one failed leader operated under the "my way or the highway" leadership style. Another participant shared one of the leaders had "no leadership style." One of the participants surprised me by revealing, "one failed leader's style was anything incongruent with the organization." Although I did not list all the weaknesses, the number of perceived weaknesses the participants shared was astonishing. I ranked the weaknesses numerically from most weak to least weak.

Interestingly, more than 50% (23 of 27 with two not responding) communicated the failed leaders had positive attributes worth mentioning. The positive attributes were diverse (e.g. voice, public speaking, academic record, and hard worker). Even though the participants were willing to share positive attributes of the leaders who failed, the participants concluded the identification of the positive attributes with negative disclaimers.

I was shocked by many of the negative disclaimers. The negative effect the failed leader had on the organization was understandable when the participants revealed the negative actions associated with the positive attributes. Employees' frustration and community negative perception are two of the most prevalent negative results.

The participants indicated lessons learned from the failed leaders that could add value to other organizations and their leadership. Three of the opinions they shared follow:

1. A leader needs to earn the respect of his peers and

subordinates.

2. Listening to others is important, and use feedback for corrective criticism.

3. It is important to be a visionary leader and to understand the concepts of new ideas, but is alsocritical to learn from mistakes.

The participants also made comments about leaders and leadership that could be useful for purposes of this study and could help reduce leadership failure. One participant concluded "the leader should not be an army of one" and that "if the leader is not connected to employees there will be a weakness."

Surprising Results

The surprise in the Brown (2005) study was that the participants were not reluctant to share information about leadership failure because of the confidentially they were promised. Many of the participants had major concerns about leadership failure in education, but did not have a medium to express their concerns. Some of the participants thanked me for taking the initiative to gain resourceful information in a non-traditional manner that could help improve leadership in educational organizations such as community college systems. Additionally, the extent that leadership failure in an educational system has been the catalyst for major public policy changes was a surprise.

Recommendations

This research confirmed that organizational leadership can be more effective if the reasons leaders fail are known and communicated (Brown, 2005). Essentially, the research data revealed that leadership failure does adversely affect organizations. The inference is that unless organizations are willing to take the necessary actions to correct the leadership problems, the problems will continue to occur. As some of the participants indicated, organizational leaders should evaluate aspects of leadership on a regular basis to include hiring, performance, influence on the organizational culture, and effect on organizational goals.

Community college leaders specifically should carefully examine the themes discovered in the Brown (2005) study. The themes could apply to colleges and organizations. By examining the themes, community college leaders should work with others to determine ways to circumvent future problems with leaders their organization hire or promote. For example, community college leaders do more in could have to do more in depth research into potential leaders' background prior to hiring. This hiring research may involve hiring human resources personnel who have considerable expertise in hiring leaders and in discerning character because, as one of the participants noted, some people have charisma when interviewing but still cannot satisfactorily perform the job. Furthermore, more training for organizational leaders about cultural differences, trust, leadership integrity, commitment, effective communication, and being a part of a team must be offered. The use of statistical and anecdotal records on leadership failure will help solidify the leadership training (Brown, 2005).

Too often for diverse reasons, training people in community colleges once on-the-job is overlooked, but training should be continual for personnel. Demands on community college leaders are the reason the leaders often do not get the leadership training needed, and ultimately, many of the leaders fail to satisfy organizational goals. The training should be specific to the problems and to the themes noted and should not be generalized. Frequently, leadership training is on effective leadership strategies as opposed to studying reasons leaders have failed and developing programs to address the problems (Brown, 2005). Organizational leaders gain benefits when they migrate to a paradigm in which they begin to implement strategies to alleviate failure in organizations ranging from leadership failure to other employee failures in organizations. When leaders continuously do things the same way, the leaders' actions are counter-productive to organizations. For purpose of this study, using the words of poet Robert Frost, *the road less traveled* can make all the difference in organizational leadership training and development.

As was determined, collecting data from a small segment of the leadership population, such as leaders in a community college system, was practical. Still, comparable information is needed from other levels of employees in the educational arena and other types of organizations. Because leaders who failed were not the target population for this study, it would be beneficial to discover if the leaders who were identified as failures would concur with the reasons given by the respondents for their failure, or would their responses significantly differ? Will there be new discovery? New and additional perspectives would add value to leadership in diverse organizations.

The participants in the study concurred with the researcher that this type of research conducted about leadership using a different approach was needed and should have a positive effect on organizational leadership. Leaders with more than 30 years of experience in the Community College system validated The Leadership Assessment Questionnaire is a worthwhile instrument to use to guide the questioning. The researcher can use the questionnaire to access reasons for failure in other jobs (e.g. middle level leaders, administrative assistants, faculty members, and other college personnel).

The question of leadership failure in this exploratory research yielded results that benefit leadership and organizational effectiveness literature. Additional studies would be beneficial to gain more insight on leadership failures. Other topics that would fill gaps in the literature on leadership failure include the following:

1. How many, if any, of the colleges in the community college systems changed policies and procedures based on the results of a leadership failure study?
2. What reasons do leaders who failed in community colleges give for their failure?
3. Do more leaders who fail in community colleges versus four year college?
4. What effect does training leaders to be successful have on their success?
5. Is there a direct correlation between leadership style and leaders who fail to satisfy organizational goals?
6. Is leadership failure more prevalent in one type organization versus another?
7. How do military organizations reduce levels of leadership failure?
8. Do leaders' years of experience have a significant impact on the possibility of leadership failure?
9. What is the failure rate of leaders based on gender? Are women or men more prone to failure or success?

Conclusion

The purpose of the Brown (2005) study was to explore some of the reasons leaders fail to satisfy organizational goals within post-secondary education with emphasis community college leaders. The major objective was met. The information gathered is resourceful, adds value to the study of leadership, and will be used to promote best practices for a successful organization. Because questions remain about the most effective ways to lead and leadership failure, leadership continues to be one of the most researched topics. Problems, such as leadership failure, must be identified. The results of research on leadership failure could astound readers. Brown's study revealed policy changes made in a community college system because of leadership failure. With every negative response about leaders' actions, a greater positive solution to the problem is possible. The absence of information on leaders may be a deterrent to the success of an organization. When leaders fail to satisfy organizational goals, the organization is adversely affected. To assist society and to increase organizational effectiveness educational organizations and researchers with expertise in leadership should take the lead in discovering reasons for leadership failure and then seek ways to reduce the possibility of failure. Educational researchers are expected to conduct research that is relevant (Sallie & Flood, 2012) in their quest to help alleviate leadership problems.

No consensus amongst scholars exists about ways to solve leadership problems. One way to rectify leadership problems and to circumvent future leadership problems in organizations is through discovery of the reasons for problems. The uncommon approach to studying leadership failure using qualitative methods in Brown (2005) study uncovered themes associated with leaders who failed. The qualitative grounded theory method will reveal essential facts when the method is properly applied. Once the problems are discovered, actions to alleviate future leadership problems should be taken. Studies have shown that knowledgeable leaders are essential to the success of any business (Phillips, 2004; Selcer, Goodman, & Decker, 2012). Conducting research on leaders and developing leaders to help reduce leadership failure to increase organizational effectiveness is imperative.

Thoughts from the Academic Entrepreneur™

The problem to be solved:

- The lack of consistency of effective leadership definitions

The goals:

- To find consensus regarding the qualities of a successful leader versus those of an unsuccessful leader.

The questions to ask:

- What are the reasons some leaders such as educational leaders, are unsuccessful in their quest to lead others when attempting to respond to organizational goals?

Today's Business Application

- Lacking leadership skills and ineffective communication are the two most often-cited reasons why leaders fail. Don't let that be you (or your managers)!
- Training should be continual for anyone in a leadership position.
- Good leaders continually balance their vision against the price of setbacks and challenges.

References

Abts, M. (2013). Effectiveness of online community college success courses. *League for Innovation in the College, 16.* Retrieved from http://www.league.org/blog/post.cfm/effectiveness-of-online-community-college-success-courses

Amey, M. J., & Van DerLinden, K. E. (2002). Career paths for community college leaders. *Research Brief Leadership Series, no. 2, AACC-RBB-02-2.* Washington, DC: American Association of Community Colleges. Retrieved from http://www.aacc.nche.edu/Publications/.../Documents/06242002careerpaths.pdf

Armstrong, T. (2009). Learning from failures in O.D. consulting. *Organization Development Journal, 27,* 71-77. Retrieved from http://hbr.org/archive-toc/BR1104

Bennis, W. (1989). *Why leaders can't lead.* San Francisco, CA: Jossey-Bass Publishers.

Bennis, W. (1997). *Herding cats.* Provo, UT: Executive Excellence Publishing.

Bennis, W. (2013). Leadership in a digital world: Embracing transparency and adaptive capacity. *MIS Quarterly, 37,* 635-636. Retrieved from http://www.misq.org/contents-37-2

Beyer, B. (2012). Blending constructs and concepts: Development of emerging theories of organizational leadership and their relationship to leadership practices for social justice. *International Journal of Educational Leadership Preparation, 7*(3). Retrieved from http://eric.ed.gov/?id=EJ997470

Birnbaum, R. (1992). *How academic leadership works.* San Francisco, CA: Jossey-Bass.

Brill, P. L., & Sloan, K. (2011). Peak performance for political leaders. *Journal of Leadership Studies, 5,* 76-83. doi:10.1002/jls.20207.

Brown, A. (2005). A study of leadership failure: Perceptions of Leaders within a community college system. *Dissertation Abstracts International, 66-07,* 2630. Retrieved from Proquest Dissertation and Theses.

Brown, P. (2011). Who's next in line:? Develop tomorrow's leaders today. *Public Manager, 40*(4), 38-41.

Burns, G., & Martin, B. N. (2010). Examination of the effectiveness of male and female educational leaders who made use of the invitational leadership style of leadership. *Journal of Invitational Theory and Practice, 16*, 30-56. Retrieved from http://www.eric.ed.gov/contentdelivery/servlet/ERICServlet?accno=EJ942556

Cohen, A. M., & Brawer, F. B. (2008). Managing community colleges: A Handbook for Effective Practice. San Francisco, CA: Jossey-Bass.

Depree, (1989). *Leadership is an art*. New York, NY: Doubleday.

Downey, D. (2001). *Assimilating new leaders: The key to executive retention*. New York, NY: AMACOM.

Drucker, P. (1996). *The leader of the future*. New York, NY: The Peter Drucker Foundation for Nonprofit Management.

Dulebohn, J. H., Bommer, W. H., Liden, R. C., Brouer, R. L., & Ferris, G. R. (2011). Leader-member exchange (LMX) and culture. A meta-analysis of correlates of LMX across 23 countries. *Journal of Applied Psychology, 97*, 1097-1130. doi:10.1177/0149206311415280

Eddy, P. L. (2013). Developing leaders: The role of competencies in rural community colleges. Community College Review, *41*, 20-43. doi:10.1177/0091552112471557

Fiedler, F. E. (1971). *Leadership*. New York, NY: General Learning Press.

Gentry, W., & Sparks, T. (2012). A convergence / divergence perspective of leadership competencies managers believe are most important for success in organizations: A cross-cultural multilevel analysis of 40 countries. *Journal of Business & Psychology, 27*, 15-30. doi:10.1007/s10869-011-9212-y

Gordon, W. (2011). Behavioural economics and qualitative research -- a marriage made in heaven? *International Journal of Market Research*. *53*, 171-185, doi:10.2501/IJMR-53-2-173-188

Green, R. L., & Cooper, T. (2012; 2013)Identification of the most preferred dispositions of effective leaders. *National Forum of Applied Educational Research Journal, 26*, 1 & 2, 55-76.

Griffin, M. A., Parker, S. K., & Mason, C. M. (2010). Leader vision and the development of adaptive and proactive performance: A longitudinal study. *Journal of Applied Psychology, 95*, 174-182. doi:10.1037/a0017263

Kaiser, R. B., Hogan, R., & Craig, S. B. (2008). Leadership and the fate of organizations. *American Psychologist, 63*, 96-110, doi:10.1037/003-066x.63.2.96

Kalaluhi, S. (2013). Leadership in context: The moderating effect of follower need for autonomy on directive leadership style, empowering leadership style, and leader effectiveness in volunteer organizations. *Global Conference on Business & Finance Proceedings, 8*, 139-143. Retrieved from http://www.theibfr.com/ARCHIVE/ISSN-1941-9589-V8-N1-2013.pdf

Katsinas, S. G., & D'Amico, M. M., & Friedel, J. N. (2012). Workforce training in a recovering economy: Perceptions of state community college leaders. Retrieved from http://www.cscconline.org/files/2413/2337/8998/College_Completion_2011_12-8-2011.pdf.

Little, G. W. (2002). Resolving the leadership crisis. *Community College Journal, 73*, 33.

McCuddy, M. K., & Cavin, M. C. (2008). Fundamental moral orientations, servant leadership, and leadership effectiveness: An empirical test. *Review of Business Research, 81*, 107-117.

Merriam, S. B. (2001). *Qualitative research and case study applications in education.* San Francisco, CA: Jossey-Bass.

Phillips, J. J. (2004). *The leadership scorecard.* Burlington, MA: Elsevier Butterworth-Heinemann.

Portnoy, R. A. (1986). *Leadership! What every leader should know about people.* Englewood Cliffs, NJ: Prentice-Hall.

Ready, D. A., & Conger, J. A. (2008). Winning the race for talent in emerging markets. *Harvard Business Review, 86,* 63. Retrieved from http://hbr.org/2008/11/winning-the-race-for-talent-in-emerging-markets/ar/1

Sakiru, O. K., D'silva, J. L., Othman, J., DaudSilong, A., & Busayo, A. T. (2013). Leadership styles and job satisfaction among employees in small and medium enterprises. doi:10.5539/ijbm.v8n13p34

Sallee, M., & Flood, J. T. (2012). Using qualitative research to bridge research, policy, and practice. *Theory into Practice, 51*, 137-144. doi:10.1080/00405841.2012.662873

Selcer, A., Goodman, G., & Decker, P. (2012). Fostering transformational leadership in business and health administration education through appreciative inquiry coaching. *Business Education Innovation Journal, 4*, 10-19.

Shenkman, (2004). Successful leaders: understanding sincere failure. *Sideroad Publications.* http://www.sideroad.com/Leadership/sincere-failure.html

Shults, C. (2001). The critical impact of impending retirements on community college leaders. *Research Brief Leadership Series, no. 1, AACC-RBB-01-5.* Washington, DC: American Association of Community Colleges. Retrieved from http://eric.ed.gov/?id=ED451833

Shushok, F., & Moore, S. H. (2010). Reading, study, and discussion of the *"great texts"* of literature, philosophy, and politics as a complement to contemporary leadership education literature. *Journal of Leadership Studies, 3*, 71-80. doi:10.1002/jls.20141

Spears, M. C., & Parker, D. F. (2013). Attributes that best describe successful leaders: A perceptual analysis. *Advances in Management, 6*, 31-36.

Tost, L. P., Gino, F., & Larrick, R. P. (2013). When power makes others speechless: The negative impact of leader power on team performance. *Academy of Management Journal, 56*, 1465, doi:10.5465/amj.2011.0180

Wolf, D. B., & Carroll, C. M. (2002). Leadership blues. *Community College Journal*, 12-17. Retrieved from http://www.ccjournal-digital.com/ccjournal/20130809?pg=32

Vidyarthi, P. R., Erdogan, B., Anand, S., Liden, R., & Chaudhry, A. (2014). One leader, two leaders: Extending leader-member exhchange theory to a dual leadership context. *Journal of Applied Psychology.* American Psychological Association, doi:10.1037/a0035466

Yukl, G. (2012). Effective leadership behavior: What we know and what questions need more attention. *Academy of Management ePerspectives, 26*, 66-85. doi:10.5465/amp.2012.0088

About the Author...

International trainer and motivational speaker Dr. Annie H. Brown holds several nationally accredited degrees: Doctor of Philosophy (Ph.D) Applied Management and Decision Science with Leadership and Organizational Change specialization from Walden University; Master of Business Administration (MBA) from Francis Marion University (FMU); Bachelor of Business Administration (BBA) with a management concentration and English cognate from FMU; Associate of Science (A.S) in Data Processing (comparable to Computer Technology) from Florence Darlington Technical College.

Dr. Annie, Chief Executive Officer of AnnBro International Training and Business Consulting, is a university professor with University of Phoenix (UOP) and Walden University. At Walden, Dr. Brown also serves as University Research Reviewer, doctoral committee chair, and faculty mentor for doctoral learners, as well as doctoral study committee member for Walden and UOP. Dr Annie offers expertise in editing professional documents (e.g. thesis, dissertations, & college accreditation documents) to include APA style. Dr. Annie is actively involved as board member and participant in many civic and community organizations.

Dr. Annie's exceptional interpersonal skills and more than 25 years training expertise are assets as she provides diverse types of training, to include leadership, teambuilding, communication, customer service, conflict resolution, personality typing, life coach, sustainability, and working with diverse generations of people. As a toastmaster certified distinguished speaker, Dr. Annie brings extraordinary enthusiasm to the stage as she speaks to audiences of all ages in varied organizations. She is very passionate about speaking to educational audiences.

Additional published works include her dissertation: *A Study of Leadership Failure: Perceptions of Leaders within a Community College System*, October 2005. She is currently conducting research on the impact of leadership failure in diverse organizations and character building.

To reach Dr. Brown for additional information and training or speaking requests, please e-mail drannbro@gmail.com

CHAPTER 7

*Effective Motivation and Communication Strategies for
Faculty in Higher Education: Blurring the Lines Between
Business and Academia*

By Dr. Neil Mathur and Dr. Cheryl Lentz

A primary goal of higher education, regardless of modality,
is for faculty to find effective methods to connect with
students to facilitate productive learning. The age-old
challenge is the question of how. Many new teaching strategies
for adult learners include the use of emerging technologies;
the integration of blogs and videos into classwork is one such
increasingly popular strategy. When students and faculty are no
longer face-to-face, and when learning is often asynchronous,
challenges exist for faculty to create effective learning communities
in the classroom to enhance student performance, productivity,
and effectiveness of learning outcomes. Thus, the purpose of
this chapter is to integrate what is known regarding theories
and principles of communication and motivation, and how to
shorten the learning curve of faculty in higher education in their
application and use in the classroom. In turn, this integration of
strategy will facilitate more effective outcomes of learning by their
students.

Transactional vs. Transformational Learning

Students have many paths to travel when in pursuit of higher education because of emerging technologies. One can pursue the traditional in-residence or brick and mortar option, a completely online option, or the hybrid opportunity—where a variety of options are present, blending an in-person, or nearly in-person option (such as Skype), with the online option. With these choices, students have many opportunities to find an educational strategy and modality that fits their lifestyle and learning preferences, and the ability to create a personal relationship with the course content. Ultimately, the student must discover which strategy meets his or her unique needs.

Leaders of institutions of higher learning must consider various business models that are effective for students, and that meet the needs of the institution. For some, a challenge emerges to select *transactional* learning (in which the student is a consumer and the professor is a customer service agent, and education is viewed as simply a purchase) or *transformational* learning (in which students enroll with the *opportunity* for learning, with the goal to help move themselves forward in their personal and professional development) (Silver & Lentz, 2012). This differentiation between transactional and transformational outlooks distinguishes whether students are consumers of education or simply educational learners.

Dependent on the *transactional* or *transformational* nature of the educational experience (in either the view of the student or school), many questions arise. First, the role of the faculty to communicate with and motivate students must be considered. Second, how motivation and communication occur in these modalities must be examined. Third, student satisfaction with instructors and courses must be considered in relation to the paradigm shift brought on by emergent technologies. The role that faculty must play regarding communication and motivation for students becomes a crucial element. Are students simply consumer learners (Silver & Lentz, 2012), where the focus is on the transactional element of learning, and in which a student enrolls at an institution of higher learning as if buying a watch where dollars are exchanged for a product or outcome? Learning becomes a transactional exchange in which the student is a consumer and the professor is a customer service agent. Conversely, can learning remain a more transformational experience whereby the student enrolls with the *opportunity* for learning, with the goal to help move them forward in their personal and professional development? How does student satisfaction fit in with the paradigm shift of emerging technologies? Furthermore, the question emerges, how does a faculty member motivate and communicate in these new modalities? Has education transitioned into the corporate world of satisfaction indices and key performance indicators? It is critical to consider whether students are valued for their ability to transform the world after graduation because of their learning, or whether the model in academia blurs into more of a business model (in which students are mostly valued for dollars and enrollment numbers). Essentially, the question to be examined closely is the end goal(s) of higher education and how students perceive their role.

Gender Differences and Factors that Improve Student Educational Satisfaction

The latest research concerning gender differences and factors that improve student educational satisfaction begins the discussion. Mathur, Bhutani, Sharma, and Gill (2011a) examined the impact of teaching styles of instructors and professors, teaching methods, and students' educational satisfaction in India. Student satisfaction issues are prevalent in the education services industry (Gill, Tibrewala, Poczter, Biger, & Mand, 2010). Sharma and

Dhande (2010) asserted that educational satisfaction is one of the most important determinants of a student's continuance / persistence in pursuit of a degree (Ladebo, 2004).

Transactional Models and Student Retention, Loyalty, and Satisfaction

Mathur, Herbert, Nagpal, and Gill (2010) defined student educational satisfaction as the extent to which students are satisfied with a) the help they receive from their professors to learn course materials, b) the quality of education, and c) the overall learning experience. Factors such as a) quality of education, b) professors' fairness to students, and c) faculty teaching styles / methods have a positive impact on student satisfaction (Guolla, 1999). Similar to the importance of satisfying customers to retain them for profit-making institutions, satisfying admitted students is important for student retention (De Shields Jr., Kara, & Kaynak, 2005; Guolla, 1999). Students are identified as customers (consumer learners) since they experience a highly valued service, potentially reinforcing the shift towards a predominantly transactional educational experience.

In an attempt to overcome challenges regarding student retention, colleges and universities support the paradigm shift offered by Silver and Lentz (2012) of students as important *customers* (Guolla, 1999). From this perspective, building relationships with students is an important strategy for improving student performance and educational satisfaction. These relationships improve student loyalty to the college and university (Mathur et al., 2011a). Therefore, the resultant thesis is that a faculty member's positive behavior and attitude towards students and the students' higher perceived performance improve student satisfaction with a college/university (Mathur et al., 2011a).

Similar to the tenets of marketing, students reporting high levels of satisfaction engage in favorable word-of-mouth communication, such as recommendations to friends or inquiring as to whether an instructor teaches another course; this increases the potential number of students applying to the school, student retention, and the school's profit (Mathur et al., 2011a). By contrast, students with low levels of satisfaction engage in negative word-of-mouth communication. However, professor teaching styles have both negative and positive influences on students' development of critical thinking skills and on their establishment of relationships with faculty and with a college or university. For example, Marks, Sibley, and Arbaugh (2005) found that instructor behavior toward students was the most important explanatory variable in their model of student satisfaction. Marks et al. (2011) targeted the population of East-Asian students who considered professors their *gurus* rather than just teachers, and this identification offers an interesting perspective regarding the transformational nature of the educational process. For instance, the social context of the classroom and faculty interaction outside the classroom reinforces the importance of student perception to Asian students' academic success (Hermans, Haytko, & Mott-Stenerson, 2009). This social context enhances student educational satisfaction with a college and university. The conclusions drawn by Marks et al. (2005) offered reflection on whether these elements are generalizable to all student populations worthy of a more in-depth study. In transactional models, students may also have unrealistic performance expectations, which may have a negative impact on their educational satisfaction. Hermans et al. (2009) explained that the expected course grade may be a better indicator of satisfaction with an individual course. Cooke, Sims, and Joseph (1995) found that students are more likely to quit school if their educational expectations are not met. Cooke et al. also found that there is an expectation of a transactional relationship. Some students paid fees and expected a specific grade outcome independent of their efforts in the classroom.

In summary, the above studies suggest that positive attitudes of teaching staff have a positive impact on student educational satisfaction (Cooke et al., 1995; Hermans et al., 2009). Using the previously discussed appropriate teaching methods improves educational satisfaction of students (Mathur et al., 2011a).

Indian Commerce Study

East-Indian commerce undergraduate communication students offer an example as a result of the Mathur, Bhutani, Culpepper, Mand, and Gill (2011) study. The perceived student educational satisfaction of Indian undergraduate commerce students relates to the improvement in the perceived positive attitudes of the immediate teaching staff towards students, the quality of instruction provided by the immediate teaching staff, appropriate teaching methods used by professors, and perceived academic performance (Mathur et al., 2011b).

Student Perceived Academic Performance (SPAP), previously discussed is a measure of student satisfaction, differed between male and female students. The male students' satisfaction related positively to the improvement in the perceived positive attitudes of the immediate teaching staff towards students, the quality of instruction provided by the immediate teaching staff, and appropriate teaching methods used by professors. However, in the case of Indian female undergraduate commerce students, satisfaction related to the improvement in the perceived positive attitudes of the immediate teaching staff towards students, the quality of instruction provided by the immediate teaching staff, and *perceived academic performance*. Although gender differences exist, higher perceived academic performance (learning) of students improves their perceived educational satisfaction (Mathur et al.,

2011b). To confront the other differences, Mathur et al. (2011b) recommended that professors ask the students in their classes which teaching styles and methods they prefer to include: a) visual learning, b) auditory learning, and c) kinesthetic learning. Based on student opinion, professors should consider adjusting their teaching styles and teaching methods to improve student learning and student academic performance (Mathur et al., 2011b). The adjustment in teaching styles and teaching methods, along with improved student perceived performance, increased student educational satisfaction, which in turn, may lead to improved student retention (Mathur et al., 2011b). Improved student retention will have a direct effect on the bottom line of colleges and universities by improving tuition fee revenues and perhaps alumni donations. This strategy is valuable for schools following transactional models to consider.

Types of Students

Student satisfaction is affected by students' financial situations. There are students who pay for their education themselves, some who require financial aid from either grants or loans, and some who finance their education via scholarships or corporate tuition reimbursement, including U.S. government offerings such as the GI Bill. The question to ask is how a student finances their education and how this choice affects motivation. The question to examine further is whether faculty need to know these elements. If known, would this information of how a student is financing his or her education affect teaching strategies and success outcomes?

One must keep in mind that financial information is part of the Family Education Rights and Privacy Act (FERPA). Therefore, it is possible that for-profit universities may need to adopt a different approach to student satisfaction than high-ranking universities granting full scholarships, where the student, rather than his or her money, provides the school with an asset. If a student earns a full scholarship, he or she will be unlikely to view the experience as transactional, but rather as transformative. As he or she is not paying for the education, the student is likely attending by his or her own wishes to transform, and the school (if the institution gives the scholarship to the student) is likely to view the student— rather than the funds of the student—as a valuable asset.

Another question to examine is whether type or level of the student affects understanding and perception of satisfaction. Student types can include undergraduate, graduate, or doctoral student designations, where this element may be an important consideration as well. There are additional questions to consider regarding type of program studied, i.e. a more practically oriented program, such as a Doctorate of Business Administration (DBA), or a more theoretically oriented program, such as a PhD. "Knox (2009) underscored that adult learners desire a praxis-oriented approach to learning that allows the individual to move back and forth between theory and application" (as cited in Woodruff & Lentz, 2012, p. 5). Considerations for learning preferences as well as the type of student and education path pursuit may have considerable impact on the concept of self-satisfaction, as further research may discover.

Again, one returns to questioning whether education is similar to employee productivity as in the corporate landscape, where one looks at factors that increase employee performance. Are students employees in this sense of transactional educational goals? Does the manner in which one labels a student or employee affect how one might integrate appropriate and more effective business strategies and productivity measures? Our discussion continues to examine the results of the following study by Crossman (2013).

Supply Chain Professionals' Motivation in South-Central Kansas

The effects of motivation on employee productivity to try to determine the factors that increase employee performance and increase business growth is a field of study and practical interest (Crossman, 2013). An element in the future business growth of a company focuses on the relationship between employee and employer (student and institutions of higher learning within academia). Employers with positive relationships with employees, and faculty with positive relationships with their students, may create work (learning) environments that encourage engagement that is more productive.

Leaders, whether in the business world or within academia, need to be aware of their communication style as they work to engage employees and students. Although pay and grades may be one method that leaders use to motivate employees, use of pay alone may not affect the motivation of all employees. Is pay comparable to how a student finances or pays for (or is paid to) attend university? Leaders need to be aware of the motivators that their employees have identified that may affect the employee's performance to tailor incentives to meet those needs. To understand the effects of motivation, leaders need to develop practices necessary to motivate employees and students. Topics include examinations of incentives within corporate policies that encourage employees to perform at their best, and review of organizational leadership strategies regarding best practices for motivating employees. Examination of research furthers this discussion as the lines continue to blur between business and institutions of higher learning.

In Crossman's (2013) study to identify attributes that support intrinsic motivation, 11% of the participants indicated the essential need for the leader to refrain from micromanaging their work, and 9% of the participants indicated personal pride when they completed a project (Crossman, 2013) Additionally, 6% of the participants stated that attitude was important to their motivation (Crossman, 2013). The 6% of the participants added that the attitude to do a good job pushed them to work hard daily (Crossman, 2013).

Communication was the next coded theme for the Crossman (2013) study regarding employee motivation. Of the participants interviewed, 18% indicated that having management tell them that they are doing a fantastic job was a motivator for them (Crossman, 2013). When telling the employee that are doing a great job, 20% liked when the manager told them in front of a group and 14% preferred that the manager tell them privately (Crossman, 2013). Additionally, 16% of the participants felt that teamwork was a motivator to meet business goals, and 10% of the participants felt that a manager communicating the company goals plus their performance in relation to those goals was motivating (Crossman, 2013). The outcomes of the interviews that support the code of communication connect back to the themes of the study conducted by Mayo at the Hawthorne plant in 1920. Mayo (1933) claimed that communication and employee attention were the keys to employee motivation.

Because of research by Crossman (2013), the following points are of importance to professional educators. If one assumes that student productivity can be advanced with more effective outcomes, the question to ask is how faculty can adjust teaching strategies to enhance student learning as a result. If company goals are considered motivating, could the question be asked whether learning outcomes as student goals would similarly motivate well within the academic setting? Do the lines blur between the corporate landscape of business (employers / employees) and academia, and apply findings to the relationship between faculty and students as well as the institutions of higher learning and their students? The question to examine is whether key performance indicators in business can be applied successfully to academic institutions in similar and comparable ways.

An additional piece of the puzzle includes the social nature of the human condition as part of the relationships of interaction. Since social needs are part of the human experience and part of Maslow's (1954) Hierarchy of Needs, the next point to consider is whether the modality of in-residence, online, or a hybrid model affects teaching strategies and subsequent student motivation as a result of the social needs of particular students. Does a correlation exist between social needs and motivational outcomes in the classroom, further affected by the chosen path or modality? The following study by Mathur and Gill (2007) provided insights on these questions regarding social influence and the influence of leadership strategies.

Improving Employee Dedication and Pro-social Behavior

Mathur and Gill (2007) examined the relationship between transformational leadership and employee dedication, and the relationship between transformational leadership and pro-social behavior. If employees perceive that their managers are using high-level transformational leadership, employee dedication and pro-social behaviour are also perceived at a higher level (Mathur & Gill, 2007). Issues of poor employee dedication and pro-social behaviour lead to other internal organizational problems—a lack of employee dedication leads to high employee turnover, resulting in higher labour costs. A lack of employee pro-social behaviour causes poor quality service to customers.

Pro-social behaviour, in this context, is the expected customer-contact service employees' (CCSE) behaviour intended to delight guests by providing little extras and spontaneous exceptional service (Mathur & Gill, 2007). In addition, employee pro-social behaviour is important to an organization as this element represents the behaviour beyond what is expected of employees to complete tasks that are essential to the hospitality organization but that are not necessarily in the formal job descriptions of the employees. Transformational Leadership (TL), as a positive force, promises to drive changes in employee attitudes to perform pro-social behaviour. Leaders, through TL traits, exhibit empathetic attitudes (Barbuto & Burbach, 2006), which in turn change CCSE mood positively to perform pro-social behaviour. Thus, Transformational Leaders' behavior has significant positive effect on CCSE's pro-social behaviour. It is theorized that CCSEs who are clearer about their organization's mission, goals, and objectives, which are the results of TL, will perform higher pro-social behaviors than those who are not clear.

A positive relationship between TL and employee dedication was found. The improvement in the degree of perceived employee dedication of CCSEs is related to the improvement in the degree of perceived TL implementation. Thus, the improvement in the degree of TL implementation improves the degree of perceived CCSEs' dedication to the hospitality organizations. In addition, TLs play an important role in increasing CCSEs' dedication to the hospitality organizations through transformational leadership.

Implementation of Transformational Leadership Approaches

There are many organizational barriers (e.g. lack of employee's understanding of the mission, goals, and objectives, communication barriers, lack of time, cultural barriers, shortage of staff, employee de-motivation, high employee turnover, managers' understanding the degree to which TL needs to be implemented, etc.) that make transformation difficult. To overcome the above challenges, hospitality managers and supervisors need to communicate the organization's mission, goals, and objectives to CCSEs by *breaking them down* for each individual employee based on the hospitality function performed. To encourage downward communication, strategies include using bulletin boards, handouts appended to employee paychecks, and thorough communication to employees to delegate responsibility. To encourage upward communication, strategies include having an open door policy (e.g. have management walking around) for employee suggestions to obtain feedback on the degree of TL implementation. Additionally, learning effective time management skills to deal with any time barriers, and having regular on-floor training and coaching, encourages employee buy-in to take on and commit to additional responsibilities. Having constant communication to reinforce the vision, mission, goals, and objectives of the organization (hotel) as well as individual department (e.g. housekeeping, front desk, food services, etc.) are also effective strategies to use. Finally, changing one's leadership style from regular to transformational through practicing new leadership skills, as well as the practice effective listening skills (e.g. show employees that you want to listen, be patient, hold your temper, go easy on argument and criticism, and ask relevant questions) to overcome communication and cultural barriers, and acting as mentors (e.g. train, advise, coach, support, and encourage) CCSEs to overcome employee de-motivation and to understand the degree and barriers to implement TL offer effective and productive outcomes. These recommendations require leaders to internalize the importance of showing genuine concern and respect for employees and their work. Since the consequences of poor employee dedication lead to other issues such as high employee turnover, and because TL is associated with higher employee dedication to the hospitality organizations and pro-social behaviour, implementing TL as the managerial method of choice is highly advocated.

The Relations of Transformational Leadership and Empowerment with Student Perceived Academic Performance: A Study among Indian Commerce Students

Although students represent an important source of revenue, they create some challenges for colleges and universities because of different learning styles. Asian students from different geographic areas have different behaviors, cultures, attitudes, and learning styles (Gill, Biger, & Dhaliwal, 2008), which lead to student leadership issues and challenges for professors (Salvarajah, 2006). When professors are unable to overcome the leadership issues, students tend to withdraw from the education program, which is not favorable for educational institutions. The higher withdrawal rates from degree programs can be a result of poor performance in the classroom and on exams in particular. Declining retention rates in institutions for higher learning is not a new problem, but one recognized as a major issue for colleges and universities (Scoggin & Styron, 2006). Lauerman (2010) indicated that almost 57% of students at 16 for-profit colleges who started classes in the 2008-2009 academic year dropped out from the education program.

Although getting more students into colleges and universities has been the top priority of India's higher education leaders for decades, the reality is that few who go to college / university finish a degree. Therefore, it is important to find strategies that improve student perceived academic performance, which in turn will help to improve student retention.

Transformational leadership and empowerment, when applied by professors, hold immense promise for colleges and universities because these concepts can be used to improve student perceived academic performance. Transformational leadership, in the context of this study, is defined as the extent to which professors motivate and encourage students to use their own judgment and intelligence to solve education-related problems, transfer missions to students, and express appreciation for good work (Gill, Tibrewala, Poczter, Biger, Mand, Sharma, & Dhande, 2010),.

Transformational leadership is used to encourage open communication with followers (Gill et al., 2010), which in turn enhances student learning in the classroom. In addition, professors using transformational leadership can clarify the goals and objectives of the course, helping students to enhance their perceived academic performance. Therefore, it is theorized that transformational leadership, where implemented, should enhance student perceived academic performance.

Student empowerment seems a logical reaction to current demands for college / university reform and accountability to student perceived academic performance. One can understand a lack of student engagement in learning, for instance, as a reaction to a lack of empowerment. Because of denied formal power in the classroom, students frequently disengage from learning (McQuillan, 2005), which has a negative impact on their academic performance.

The empowered students develop ability, confidence, and motivation to succeed academically (Cummins, 1986). McQuillan (2005) indicated that the empowered students internalize higher-level cognitive skills and assume greater control over setting their own learning goals, thereby improving student perceived academic performance. Gondal and Khan (2008) found a positive relationship between team empowerment and team performance, and Abbas and Yaqoob (2009) found a positive relationship between empowerment and employee performance.

If knowledge is power, it seems reasonable to assume that

colleges and universities should be empowering students to improve their perceived academic performance. While few would deny this assertion, *student empowerment* may be one of the most important tools to improve student perceived academic performance. Therefore, it is theorized that student empowerment, where implemented, should show improved student perceived academic performance.

Although transformational leadership enhances the students' perceived academic performance, there are some barriers that can make implementation of transformational leadership approaches (e.g., lack of student's understanding of the course goals and objectives, communication barriers, lack of time, cultural barriers, instructors' understanding the degree to which transformational leadership needs to be implemented, etc.) difficult (Gill et al., 2010, p. 7).

To overcome these challenges, faculty need to communicate the course goals and objectives to students by *breaking them down* for each individual student. Faculty should foster upward and downward communication. Practicing effective listening skills (e.g., showing students that you want to listen, being patient, holding your temper, going easy on argument and criticism, and asking relevant questions) can go a long way toward demonstrating respect and concern for students' personal feelings as well as overcoming communication and cultural barriers. Ultimately, faculty should act as mentors (e.g., educate, advise, coach, support, and encourage) to students to fully realize the degree to which transformational leadership needs to be implemented (Mathur & Gill, 2007).

These findings require faculty to internalize the importance of showing genuine concern and respect for students and their learning styles. In practice, although it may be difficult for some faculty members to increase their use of authentic communication and these transformational leadership behaviors, and although some students may eye a change in teaching styles with skepticism, the potential benefits far outweigh the costs, and such behaviors are developmental. The importance of such a leadership development process, however, must be championed and strongly supported by senior leadership and academic leaders such as a Dean or Program Director (Gill et al., 2010, p. 8).

Empowerment is a *bottom-up* process rather than something formulated as a *top-down* strategy. It is highly recommended that faculty implement transformational leadership before empowering students because this sequence will clarify the educational mission, goals, and objectives. In addition, universities and colleges must train faculty, clarify the responsibilities, and provide clear direction to the empowered employees. It is also important to find student desire for empowerment before empowering them. Faculty should learn to trust students, provide frequent feedback, and make students feel recognized for empowered behavior (Mathur & Gill, 2007).

If Indian commerce students perceive that their professors are using a high level of transformational leadership, their academic performance is perceived as at a higher level than if it is perceived as being used at lower level. If Indian students perceive that they are empowered at a higher level, their academic performance is perceived as at a higher level than if it is perceived as being used at lower level.

Finally, a discussion regarding the pursuit of higher education would not be complete without examining education or completion rates (graduation). Motivation must examine the idea of what it takes to complete pursuit of higher education. Why do some students sail through a program, while others never finish? Can we once again relate and blur the lines between education and the business world regarding what is known about why employees quit in the business world? Are there lessons faculty can integrate as part of overcoming these barriers to help motivate students to complete their education?

Conclusion

This chapter began with identifying the goals of higher education, where regardless of modality, faculty interest includes the most effective way to connect with their students to facilitate effective and productive learning. The age old dilemma this chapter focused on was the question of how, supporting the tenets of the refractive thinking, challenging conventional wisdom. Were there lessons from the business world that one could use to blur the lines between academia and business, between students as consumers and employees? When students and faculty are no longer face-to-face, and when learning is often asynchronous, the faculty is challenged with how to create effective learning communities in the classroom to enhance student performance, productivity, and effectiveness of learning outcomes. The purpose of this chapter was to offer the reader the ability to integrate what is known regarding theories and principles of communication and motivation to shorten the learning curve of faculty in higher education to facilitate more effective outcomes of learning by students and to further the aims of thinking beyond boundaries.

Thoughts from the Academic Entrepreneur™
The problem to be solved:
- How to find effective methods to connect with students to facilitate productive learning despite emerging technologies and new research

The goals:
- To shorten the learning curve of faculty in higher education in their application and use in the classroom

of effective theories and principles of communication and motivation to facilitate more effective outcomes of learning by their students..

The questions to ask:

- How can lessons learned in the business world facilitate more effective learning outcomes in academia?

Today's Business Application

- Engaging students and engaging employees are goals that are not as different as one might think. Be aware of students' or employees' motivations.
- Communication and attention are the keys to motivation—but be careful; some people prefer public attention while others shy away from public attention.
- When practicing any new leadership skill, be especially present and open to feedback to see if this new practice works or not.

References

Abbas, Q., & Yaqoob, S. (2009). Effects of leadership development on employee performance in Pakistan. *Pakistan Economic and Social Review, 47,* 269-292. doi:10.5829/idosi.mejsr.2012.11.10.741

Barbuto, J. E. Jr., & Burbach, M. E. (2006). The emotional intelligence of transformational leaders: A field study of elected officials. *The Journal of Social Psychology, 146*(1), 51-64. Retrieved from http://www.tandfonline.com

Cooke, D. K., Sims, R. L., & Joseph, P. (1995). The relationship between graduate student attitudes and attrition. *The Journal of Psychology, 129,* 677-688. doi:10.1080/00223980.1995.9914938

Crossman, W. (2013). *Supply chain professionals' motivation in a South-Central Kansas aerospace manufacturing company* (Unpublished doctoral dissertation). Walden University, Minneapolis.

De Shields Jr., O.W., Kara, A., & Kaynak, E. (2005). Determinants of business student satisfaction and retention in higher education: Applying Herzberg's two-factor theory. *The International Journal of Education Management. 19*(2), 128-139. doi:10.1108/09513540510582426

Guolla, M. (1999) Assessing the teaching quality to student satisfaction relationship: Applied customer satisfaction research in the classroom. *Journal of Marketing Theory and Practice 7*(3), 87-98. Retrieved from http://www.jmtp-online.org/

Hermans, C. M., Haytko, D. L., & Mott-Stenerson, B. (2009). Student satisfaction in web-enhanced learning environments. *Journal of Instructional Pedagogies, 1,* 1-19.

Ladebo, O. J. (2004). Relationship between agricultural trainees' performance and satisfaction with academic program. *Journal of Agricultural Education and Extension, 11*(1), 55-60. doi:10.5191/jiaee.2004.11106

Lauerman, J. (2010, September 10). Dropout rate at 16 for-profit colleges was 57%. *Bloomberg News.* Retrieved from http://www.bloomberg.com

Marks, R. B., Sibley, S. D., & Arbaugh, J. B. (2005). A structural equation model of predictors for effective online learning. *Journal of*

Management Education, 29, 531-563. doi:10.1177/1052562904271199

Mathur, N., & Gill, A. (2007). Improving employee dedication and socially oriented behavior. *International Journal of Contemporary Hospitality Management, 19,* 328-334. Retrieved from http://www.emeraldinsight.com

Mathur, N., Bhutani, S., Sharma, S., & Gill, A. (2011a). The relations of empowerment and transformational leadership with employee intentions to quit: A study of restaurant workers in India. *International Journal of Management, 28(2),* 217-229. Retrieved from http://www.internationaljournalofmanagement.co.uk

Mathur, N., Bhutani, S., Culpepper, A., Mand, H., & Gill, A. (2011b). The relationship of transformational leadership and empowerment with student perceived academic performance: A study among Indian commerce students. *Business & Economics Journal, 34,* 1-9. Retrieved from http://astonjournals.com/bej

Mathur, N., Culpepper, A., & Gill, A. (2011c). The effects of empowerment and job satisfaction on employee intentions to quit: A study among Canadian hotel and restaurant employees. *Res Manageria, 2(5),* 19-26. Retrieved from http://www.assobp.org/scientiapublication

Mathur, N., Herbert, G., Nagpal, V., & Gill, A. (2011d). Gender differences and factors that improve student educational satisfaction: A study among Indian commerce students. *Res Manageria, 2(5),* 27-37. Retrieved from http://www.assobp.org/scientiapublication

Mayo, E. (1933). *The human problems of an industrial civilization.* New York, NY: The Macmillan Company.

Silver, G., & Lentz, C. (2012). *The consumer learner: Emerging expectations of a customer service mentality in post-secondary education.* Las Vegas, NV: Pensiero Press.

Woodruff, T., & Lentz, C. (2012). Social responsibility of doctoral scholars. In C Lentz (Ed.), *The refractive thinker© Vol. VII: Social responsibility* (Chapter 1, pp. 1-12). Las Vegas, NV: The Refractive Thinker Press.

About the Author...

International Best Selling author Dr. Cheryl A. Lentz, known as *The Academic Entrepreneur™*, holds several accredited degrees; a Bachelor of Arts (BA) from University of Illinois, Urbana-Champaign; a Master of Science in International Relations (MSIR) from Troy University; and a Doctorate of Management (DM) in Organizational Leadership from the University of Phoenix School of Advanced Studies. She has her Sloan C Certification from Colorado State University–Global, as well as her Quality Matters Peer Reviewer (APP/PRC) Certification.

Dr. Cheryl, affectionately known as 'Doc C' to her students, is a university professor on faculty with Embry-Riddle University, University of Phoenix, The University of the Rockies, and Walden University. Dr. Cheryl serves as a dissertation mentor/chair and committee member. She is also a dissertation coach, offering expertise as a professional editor for APA style for graduate thesis and doctoral dissertations, as well as faculty journal publications and books.

Dr. Cheryl is also an active member of Alpha Sigma Alpha Sorority.

She is a prolific author known for her writings on *The Golden Palace Theory of Management* and refractive thinking. Additional published works include her dissertation: *Strategic Decision Making in Organizational Performance, Journey Outside the Golden Palace, The Consumer Learner, Technology That Tutors, Effective Study Skills*, International Best Seller: *The Expert Success Solution*, and contributions to the award winning series: *The Refractive Thinker®: Anthology of Doctoral Learners, Volumes I-VIII*.

To reach Dr. Cheryl Lentz for information on refractive thinking, professional editing, or guest speaking, please visit her website: http://www.DrCherylLentz.com or e-mail: drcheryllentz@gmail.com

Author...

Dr. Neil Mathur

Photo and bio unavailable at the time of publishing this book.

CHAPTER 8

Implementation of New TQM Programs, Communications, and Adapting to Change

By Dr. Leo Fleming-Farrell, Dr. Elmer Hall,
and Dr. Judy Fisher-Blando

"The aim of leadership should be to improve the performance of man and machine, to improve quality, to increase output, and simultaneously to bring pride of workmanship to people"
(Deming, 2000, p. 248).

The goal of this writing is to address the management of change that is fundamental to ongoing quality. Clear communication is critical and motivating participants is essential. By the very nature of their existence, improvement programs (IPs) are central to the evolution, change, and growth of organizations. The program for quality can be a formal program as generally represented by the Total Quality Program (TQM) concept. Quality programs contribute to disruptive changes as well as incremental changes. TQM programs often excel at incremental changes, usually at the lower level of an organization (Kulach, 2013); however, the adaptation of TQM programs at the strategic organizational level and for disruptive change - such as the introduction of an IP program, have not been as successful as TQM programs aimed at incremental changes within organizations (Fleming-Farrell, 2013). Unfortunately, if the introduction of a quality program is not successful, the anticipated quality and planned efficiencies for the organizations are not gained from the program. Consequently, implementation of another IP program becomes far more difficult.

This article includes the introduction of IP programs from both an organizational perspective (from the top as a major change), as well as from the practitioner perspective (from the bottom as an incremental change). Although the focus is on TQM issues, the chapter has much broader implications to the system paradigms of the entire organization, to the transformational versus transactional aspects of leadership, as well as, to the motivation of employees. With a concentrated effort given to organizational culture, management support, leadership, and trust within the organization, areas of concerns such as a lack of motivation, negative attitudes, uncertainty regarding personal relationships, and an increased workload within the organization would cease to be obstacles to facilitate and improve change initiatives within an organization (Connell & Fisher-Blando, 2013, Robbins & Judge, 2011). The topics covered are:

- Leadership Success (and Failure) Related to Projects (and TQM).
- Refractive Thinking: Theory to Practice and Back
- Change Management within TQM Programs
- Implications of TQM Communication and Behavior
- Motivation within TQM Environments
- Benefits of Improvement Program (Six Sigma) Participation
- TQM is disconnected from Top-Level Planning
- Opportunities for Sustainable TQM Communications and Motivation
- Conclusions

Leadership Success (and Failure)
Related to Projects (and TQM)

Before discussing the more academic aspects of IP programs, a case study at Florida Power & Light (FP&L) will demonstrate a real-live business case related to the implementation of TQM at an organization. The FP&L case is a way of refractive thinking, demonstrating the academic issues and the factors associated with introduction of TQM in practice.

Continuous Improvement Case: FP&L
and Deming Award Story

In the late 1980s, Hall was a consultant at Florida Power & Light (FP&L), a subsidiary of NextEra Energy, Inc., formerly FP&L Group. At the initiative of Chief Executive (CEO) Officer John Hudiburg, FP&L undertook a an intensive, 1-year implementation of a Quality Improvement Program (QIP) with the help of Japanese consultants. This process was a full circle because leaders learned management science from Dr. W. Edwards Deming and other U.S. experts during the rebuilding of Japan after WWII. The Japanese give an award of excellence named for Deming (FP&L, n.d.). FP&L would be the first U.S. firm to achieve the *Deming Award for Quality Excellence*. Thus, the Quality Improvement Program (QIP) was born at FP&L. Other names for QIP include Continuous Quality Improvement (CQI), Total Quality Management (TQM), *Kaizen*, and International Standards Organization (ISO) standards like ISO 9000 (ISO, n.d.). In 1989, FP&L became the first non-Japanese company in the world to receive the prestigious *Deming Prize of Quality Excellence*, a quality award administered by the Union of Japanese Scientists and Engineers (JUSE) (FP&L, n.d.).

The push to implement a completely new management program at FP&L within about a year was tremendous. Secretaries spent much of their time learning statistics and producing control charts. People in the field spent nights and weekends producing charts and explaining out-of-control points. There was a **complete burnout!** . . . Even before receiving the Deming Award, Hudiburg retired. Broadhead, the CEO and President of FP&L Group decreed that *any acceptable* management process could be used by departments; they were free to use QIP, or not (Wiesendanger, 1993). Sadly, the less-than-successful implementation of QIP was a major opportunity lost. The backlash against a major change in general, and against specifically quality improvement programs, is common (Davila, Epstein, & Shelton, 2006; Leban & Stone, 2008; Maurer, 2009, 2011; Palmer, Dunford, & Akin, 2009; Weymann, 2001).

Refractive Thinking: Theory to Practice and Back

The grand theories of organizational design summarized by Scott and Davis (2007) categorized organizations into *rational* vs. *natural* and *closed* vs. *open* systems. Scientific management, would work best in a rational-closed system such as a continuous production factory, with statistical process control and continuous improvement. On the other extreme would be the natural-open systems thinking that is more focused on the human factors of management (Pfeffer & Salancik, 1978; Weick, 1969), which is more open and dynamic (Scott, 2003). Elton Mayo's (1949) findings are represented as a natural but closed system model. TQM works well in the factory environment were quantifiable data is collected for problem detection and where incremental Plan-Do-Check-Act changes can effectively be monitored. Different divisions of the same organization might have completely different systems models, the factory might be rational-closed and sales might be natural-open.

Six Sigma (*6s*) is the statistical assurance that there is a 99.9999998% of being error-free; the often cited **3.4 defects per million** limit is *4.5s*, while *6s* **is** 2 defects per billion (Six Sigma, 2013). Once humans are involved, such as handcrafted production, the statistical achievement of Six Sigma (*6s*), error-free production is not possible, realistic, or even necessary. The Six Sigma and Lean Six Sigma quality programs developed and promoted by Motorola, GE and others do not aim for near-perfect production in all cases, but in many processes especially those with outside factors and human involvement – maybe the 80-20 rule, might work best. Pareto (1906) applied an 80-20 rule, also known as the Pareto Principle, to economics in 1906 and generalized by Juran in the late 1940s. TQM attempts to apply tools that work best in each situation; but the monitoring of ongoing processes like a production line, will usually use statistical process controls, i.e., control charts.

TQM programs focus around quality teams. Robbins and Judge (2011) offered a summary of teams, team dynamics, and communications. TQM analysis and decision-making are in quality team, usually at the lower levels of the organization. Because employees involved in the process work in teams, those quality work groups usually are most informed to make improvement recommendations and assist with incremental improvements. Recommendations from work groups usually percolate up the organization one of two levels for management approval. However, top leaders of the organization make more strategic decisions. These would often be major decisions, such as opening operations in a new country or initiating a new product line. Unfortunately, companies often disconnect strategic planning and the quality management programs. Hall and Hinkelman (2013) integrated the planning necessary for a high-tech company, including the horizon planning at the top and the product pipeline (and patent protection) at the bottom. This process matches the top-down planning with the bottom-up planning into an integrated planning process. Hall and Hinkelman suggested using scenario planning to jump-start a TQM cycle in new areas or when moving into disruptive areas of innovation. The processes proposed by Hall and Hinkelman helped to bridge the gap between high-level planning and the more incremental, lower level, planning achieved by the TQM program.

Many factors influence the effectiveness of an organization and leadership, and the factors could be different before, during or after a major change, including organizational structure, specialization, complexity of the environment, boundaries, span of control, centralization, and geographic area (Jones, 2010; McAuley, Duberley, & Johnson, 2007; Robbins & Judge, 2011; Scott & Davis, 2007). Research about leadership included characteristics of leaders, task structure, initiating and influencing factors (Yukl, 2013). The leadership styles that work best depend primarily on the task environment, as well as the characteristics and strengths of the specific leader (Robbins & Judge, 2011; Yukl, 2013). "The behavioral approach has narrowed leadership into task-oriented (initiating structure) and people-oriented (consideration) styles" (Robbins & Judge, 2011, p. 439). Charismatic and transformational leadership have the most empirical support as effective leadership types (Robbins & Judge, 2011; Yukl, 2013). Ethical, servant, spiritual, and authentic leadership have less empirical support regarding effectivity; however, these theories are not necessarily exclusive of transformational and charismatic leadership types (Yukl, 2013). Ethical and trusted leaders can have very strong and loyal followers. Hall and Knab (2012) discussed the need for *sustainable leaders* to rise to the necessity of sustainability using an integrated triple-bottom line approach with combined transformational and servant leadership approaches.

TQM, conversely, is a hands-on approach to management, especially task oriented and lower-level management. Quality teams are typically self-directed groups, dealing with very real problems in the very real world . . . far from the theories of system models, TQM quality teams deal every day with change and change management, although, mostly incremental changes, i.e. continuous improvement. One change that is disruptive and critical is the decision to introduce, or change, the quality improvement program.

Change Management Associated with TQM Programs

New improvement programs could return mixed results to organizations. Organizations that implemented effective communication strategies, practices, and are *change friendly* are successful to change improvement programs. Many organizations are not successful. Higher-level managers are more satisfied with TQM program introductions than subordinate layers of the organization. International business research indicated that communication of the expectations of results has some effect on the engagement the workforce with TQM and change. Companies that persist with quality programs and do not develop those programs often are not successful; leaders could be *playing it too safe* with limited change. Encouraging employees is a primary element of communication, or at the very least, a component of communication. People become involved in the process of change. For a small business or corporate enterprise, this engagement is necessary for business development and continuous improvement, and successful leadership.

TQM is an integrated, systematic, organization-wide strategy to continuously improve products, services, and processes of an organization (Mehra, Hoffman, & Sirias, 2001). TQM represents widely accepted management practices and principles embraced by many organizations (Dean & Bowen, 1994). Given TQM's production-oriented history (Deming, 1986), organizational change could influence TQM implementation, and vice-versa.

Increasingly, leaders are interested in the leaner and more responsive operations along with reduction in cycle time to improve performance across an entire business network (Seth & Gupta, 2005). The rate of change for TQM-type programs across an array of organizations remains unabated. Over an 80-year period beginning in 1920s, 23 improvement programs associated with quality and change management were used by organizations (Carr & Johansson, 1995). According to Fleming-Farrell (2013), the rate of change increased from 10 improvement program (IP) s in a 45-year span to 15 IPs in a 25- year span. Improvement programs include various types of improvement linked to gaining competitive advantage. Foster (2007) suggested that the business reasons for the selection of specific manufacturing and quality management improvement programs are determined by the desire of the firm to improve cash flow, earnings, and productivity. However, a key feature associated with the introduction of an improvement program is the link to high failure rates of such programs. Forty percent of major changes were not successful in U.S. based companies (Maurer, 2009, 2011).

The desire by organizations to have improvement programs is evident from the literature (Fleming-Farrell, 2013). However, the mechanism for the successful implementation of the improvement programs remains elusive for many of the programs. Many of the improvement programs evolved to include some element of Six Sigma, lean six sigma, and balanced scorecard (BSC). In a 2013 study by Fleming-Farrell, the top five reasons for change are standardization of the business process, waste reduction program, improve profitability, reduce customer complaints, and improve return on investments.

However, the satisfaction ratings among the organizational layers indicated that the upper layers of the organization scored higher satisfaction ratings for the improvement program than the lower layers of the organization (Fleming-Farrell, 2013). The findings highlight the different perceptions of IP among the organizational layers. A possible reason for the apparent satisfaction-rating anomaly could be linked to the effect of the IP on the individual job function. In essence, the lower layers of the organization may not identify with the reasons for IP introduction. In situations in which such alienation occurs, more efficient communication among the organizational layers seems merited.

Newer models of quality programs include *Six Sigma* and a variant more agile called *lean six sigma* (Wedgewood, 2007). These new *flavors* of TQM are incremental and not usually the first introduction of an IP to the organization. These newer approaches to quality might not have the same degree of disconnect between higher-level managers' satisfaction and lower level employees' dissatisfaction as identified by Fleming-Farrell (2013). According to AlSagheer (2011), the Six Sigma model provides various types of sustainability to companies regarding quality and market share enhancement, zero defect level, financial returns, and optimal production level. AlSagheer suggested multinational companies find more value in Six Sigma implementation than small-scale organizations, in large part because of the enormous financial investment involved. Adopted by Motorola, Six Sigma became popular with multinational corporations, and large scale organizations (AlSagheer, 2011). Six Sigma is a multidimensional approach for improving process efficiency and attaining sustainability. This sustainability serves as a guide for smaller companies to improve efficiency and effectiveness in their markets (AlSagheer, 2011). An organization must undergo a transformational phase with proper guidelines to change from its traditional management approach to supply chain quality (Chu-Hua, Madu, & Chinho, 2008). This transformation requires visionary leadership, supporting infrastructures and climates, endorsements of suppliers, systematic change actions as outlined in Deming's Plan–Do–Check–Act cycle, and implementing improvement strategies through projects and audits (Chu-Hua et al., 2008).

Changes interact on three significant elements of the organization: the workforce in the organization, the end use of the product or service, and the leadership of the organization. Significant change and focus on IPs by the organization will require the organizational leadership to implement three actions communicate a vision to the participants, execution of a plan with the participants, and identify the change implementation deadline. Management's lack of effective communication to the workforce was cited as the primary reason for change failures (Richardson & Denton, 1996). According to Yukl (2013), leadership is a process that seeks to exert influence. The leadership process supports the performance process; however, a group of participants shares the undertaking and the mission. Leadership's ability to communicate across all strands of the organization will be of paramount importance in the leadership and management of change (Yukl, 2013).

Linked to the behavioral aspects of the management of change are communication and appreciation of the inter relationships between the elements for the change. Fleming-Farrell (2013) argued that the linkage connecting the elements of transactional, transformational leadership, TQM, and change is continual improvement. In the continual improvement environment, some element of uncertainty exists for the stakeholders. Bacha (2010) articulated the view that the perceived charismatic vigorous style of the leader has an effect on the firm's performance in environments where uncertainty existed. Transactional leaders might work well in a factory setting, but not necessarily in a dynamically changing environment. The concepts of transformational, visionary, motivational, trustfulness and leadership characteristics are linked to charismatic style (Yukl, 2013). A balanced scorecard (BSC) is a form of organizational level goal setting (Kaplan & Norton, 1996). The balanced scorecard translates the organization's vision and mission into specific, measurable performance goals related to financial, customer, internal goals and objectives, and learning and growth processes (McShane & Von Glinow, 2013). The use of a BSC in TQM helps to capture the full range of organizational performance.

Implications of TQM Communication and Behavior

The process of change can motivate, de-motivate, and alienate people; several reasons for improvement program failures have been attributed to work force disengagement, lack of communication, fear of the unknown and links to resistance to change (Yukl, 2013). Weymann (2001) cited Thorndike law (1911) of effect as the motivator for people's behavior with respect to resistance to change. In essence, if the individual does not see any benefit to him or her then a person is less likely to perform a task or meet an objective. Individual sources of resistance to change will most likely be from selective information processing (Robbins & Judge, 2011). Although an organization has guidelines and rules regarding the use of new systems, employees may hear this information selectively. This situation can lead to employees interpreting the changes to meet their own agendas. Structural inertia can also be a source of resistance from the organizational side (Rungtusanatham, 2008). The changes could affect the set manner in which employees perform duties. Some employees may not welcome the changes to the previously set methods. This can cause a natural resistance to the changes in company procedures.

In short, creating an environment that is *change friendly* is not easy.

In the context of TQM, top management involvement can take the form of transformational leadership (Dean & Bowen, 1994), which encourages values regarding change, employee empowerment and recognition, coaching and personal development (Anderson, Rungtusanatham, & Schroeder, 1994; Zairi, 1994). TQM and transformational leadership objectives emphasize the importance that leadership must set a vision and mission for employees, involve staff at appropriate levels of decision-making, and realign an organization in times of change (Wehnert, 2009). Practical implications for applying TQM practices for executives and leaders during change in an organization should include a stepwise TQM implementation approach based on the cultural values of the employees (Farrell-Fleming, 2013).

Barriers to effective communication through changes can be filtering, selective perception, and emotions. Filtering is the distortion or withholding of information to manage another person's reactions. Selective perception is a result of the often unconscious filtering process. ***Emotional disconnects*** can happen when the speaker or the listener is upset, whether about the subject matter or an unrelated incident that may have happened previously (George & Jones, 2011). Effective communication in TQM and transformation leadership requires employees to be open to speaking and listening to one another, despite possible differences in opinion or personalities.

The measurement of satisfaction from different respondent groups across organizations indicated that the higher-level layers of the organization expressed higher satisfaction with the current IP program than the subordinate layers. Fleming- Farrell (2013) indicated that satisfaction ratings had a range of values with the highest of 81% to a low of 2.7% across the hierarchical stakeholder groups. A feature of the high scoring satisfaction ratings was the association with the hierarchical group's perception of the IP benefit to the target organization performance. Thus, indicating that the communication of the potential benefits of the IP to lower layers of the hierarchy may improve satisfaction among the hierarchical stakeholder groups.

Motivation Within TQM Environments

Maslow's (1954) hierarchy groups needs into levels and highlights that the lowest needs are initially most important, but higher needs become more important as lower needs are satisfied (McShane & Von Glinow, 2013). Maslow proposed that human beings have five universal needs to satisfy: psychological needs, safety needs, belongingness needs, esteem needs, and self-actualization needs. Leaders can satisfy the needs of employees in many ways, and once sustenance needs are met, higher level needs become more important as a motivation. Maslow argued that satisfying the employees' needs should match with the organization achievement of its goals. Lower-level needs are more extrinsic, such as housing and meals (or the salary to buy necessities). Higher level needs, such as self-esteem, are encouraged by providing primarily intrinsic rewards, such as special recognition awards and programs for outstanding accomplishments and achievements (George & Jones, 2011).

Clayton Alderfer's (1972) ERG theory is also based on needs, but differs from Maslow's (1954) theory, because ERG collapses Maslow's five needs categories into three: existence needs (a desire for psychological and material well-being), related needs (desire for satisfying interpersonal relationships), and growth needs (an intrinsic desire for continued personal growth and development). Alderfer emphasized a unique *frustration-regression* component, figuring that the employees continually frustrated in their growth needs related to this needs would surface. Unlike Maslow's theory,

ERG theory contends that more than one need can be activated at the same time (Schermerhorn, Uhl-Bien, Hunt, & Osborn, 2011). As Yukl (2010) stated, "The criteria used as the basis for allocating tangible rewards signal what is valued by the organization . . . Failure to recognize contributions and achievements sends a message that they are not important" (p. 328). Deming (1986) cautioned against rewards from processes over which employees have no control because the incentive process could dispirit employees. Variable pay, like bonuses, can be an effective motivator (Robbins & Judge, 2011). Research indicated that profit sharing, gainsharing, and pay-for performance generally result in a positive effect on performance, however consistency of a reward system is critical (Yukl, 2013).

Benefits of Improvement Program
(Six Sigma) Participation

In 2013, Kulach conducted a study of Six Sigma practitioners. Kulach (2013) was intrigued by the lack of research demonstrating a benefit to the Six Sigma practitioner involved in TQM programs, although the evidence is clear that most companies benefit from TQM programs (Kulach, 2013). Kulach found that Six Sigma practitioners gained some compensation benefits from training and the exercise of quality skills. Kulach investigated the relative importance of education, industry experience, and Six Sigma training at three stages of 90 Six Sigma practitioners' careers. At the beginning of their career, education was not very important, but more relevant in compensation than Six Sigma participation and industry experience. At mid-career, the three were statistically correlated to compensation with Six Sigma participation (0.344), work experience (0.297), and education (0.281). At the current career stage, there was an increase in the value of work experience and Six Sigma training related to compensation, with correlations of 0.508 and 0.449, respectively. Education dropped in importance of to an insignificant 0.116. Also, a cross correlation existed between Six Sigma experience and Industry Experience (0.462) implying that the work on Six Sigma projects resulted in substantial cross department experience and industry knowledge. These results match with a typical career path: education (95% had bachelor's degrees or higher), obtain the first career-type job, work for some years, then start Six Sigma involvement. When asked what contributed to their current compensation (out of 100% total), participants answered on average that years of experience has a 45.34% effect, education 35.21%, and Six Sigma training a 19.44% effect to current compensation.

The Kulach (2013) study had profound implications pertaining to compensation and motivation. Average salaries for Six Sigma and lean practitioners were about $83,000 annually with less than $4,000 in bonuses. The compensation does seem to be in line with the benchmarks Kulach found at Salary.com and GlassDoor. com. Of the 90 respondents, more than half had bonuses of less than $1,500 (Kulach, 2013). Generally, less than 5% of the total compensation for the panelists came in the form of bonuses, and many had bonuses of $0 to $500 (less than 1% of their salary). Statistically, Kulach (2013) found only the involvement in Black Belt projects was weakly positively, associated with bonuses. Other factors that had no correlation were: participation in Six Sigma projects, years of experience, Green Belt Projects, and Lean Projects. Why are bonuses so weakly and inconsistently applied to the employees involved in the TQM process?

Kulach's (2013) findings could be described as completely different perspectives: the higher level management's view and the view from the Six Sigma participant. Higher-level management's view might look like this:

- Base salary is sufficient . . . It is already your job, you don't need bonuses to do the job you are already paid to complete.
- Intense company and industry expertise is expanded based on participation.
- Company (generally) pays for the Six Sigma training (again), so there is a huge investment in upgrades to human capital already.
- Six Sigma participation improves employment skills and promotion opportunities.
- The Six Sigma practitioner's view, on the other hand, might look more like this:
- Improved skills improve salary prospects within the current company and at other companies.
- Intrinsically rewards such as awards and recognition are nice, but inconsistently awarded.
- Bonuses are weak or non-existent. (I made lots of money for company: how about a little for me?)
- Black Belts (and higher) can expect to have small bonuses, although the bonuses seem to be inconsistent.
- Green, lean and participation should not expect much, if any, bonus compensation.

This scenario appears to be a *disincentive* situation. Inconsistent rewards are offered to employees whose skill sets are in high demand, while their increasing skills, company knowledge, and industry experience make them increasingly valuable to other companies.

Opportunities for Sustainable TQM Communications and Motivation

Opportunities from a review of the literature combined with the findings from Farrell-Fleming (2013) and Kulach (2013) are:

- The planning processes for most companies needs to have a better integration of high-level strategic planning with the TQM and processes.
- The effective introduction of IP programs is critical! A major failed initiative can "restrain the opportunity" for initiatives. Disillusioned employees will be less trusting and less open to the next great idea.
- Leaders need to communicate clearly, for both major and minor change initiatives. A successful implementation of QIP at FP&L resulted in the approach being rejected because of the way it was forced on employees and the failure of management to effectively communicate the importance.
- Quality programs are the most critical of all initiatives that an organization might introduce, and consequently the programs are even more critical for successful implementation. Even when implemented, however, the TQM program still requires substantial *care and feeding*.
- Engaging people in the change process is a natural part of TQM. Consequently, TQM should be a subset of effective leadership.
- Engaging people in implementation is a natural part of TQM. Consequently, TQM participants should be actively involved in the decisions that affect them to the extent practical and possible.
- Tying people's rewards to the success TQM projects seems to be a missing link.

- HR review and compensation systems should be integrated with TQM programs to match individual's rewards with project successes (and organizational performance) that are fair and equitable to all stakeholders.

Leaders who intend to market a new product, process and maintain stakeholder engagement with the change program will need to develop a good strategy for communication and excel at motivation. The effective execution of the TQM/IP concept should be a part of the leadership strategy to ensure that success is an outcome of the improvement initiative. The leaders should also look at internal and external opportunities, threats, and also strengths and weakness.

Conclusion

With proper TQM implementation, leaders and refractive thinkers can implement changes, strengthen the company's structure, enhance communication, and boost productivity while maintaining the goals and commitment to serving its customers. This focus will help the leaders develop a company culture higher in trust and participation. Implementing change appropriately will boost employee satisfaction and present a positive outcome for the company on many levels. Effective and successful change is achieved and sustained with stakeholder participation throughout the layers of the organization. Many organizations and their leaders have not given significant attention to the effects of poor communication on the sustainability of improvement programs. Evidence of the lack of sustainability is in the apparent failure of leadership to recognize and implement an effective reward and benefit concept. The goal to successful implementation of Improvement Programs and TQM type programs will rely on the ability of the organizations' leaders to communicate, to motivate, and to create satisfaction among stakeholders.

Thoughts from the Academic Entrepreneur ™

The problem to be solved:

- The challenge of improvement programs such as TQM regarding the effects of change management.

The goals:

- To address the challenges regarding the management of change that are fundamental to ongoing quality; regarding communication and motivation.

The questions to ask:

- How can improvements be made to the adaptation of TQM programs at the strategic organizational level aimed at incremental changes within organizations?

Today's Business Application

- Reward employees who generate income for the company in a consistent manner. Inconsistency is a disincentive.
- A failed internal plan can dangerously paralyze a company with the fear of change. Plan carefully and accordingly.
- Rewarding employees for the successful implementation of new workplace practices is one of the best ways to ensure they succeed.

References

Alderfer, C. P. (1972). *Existence, relatedness, and growth.* New York, NY: Free Press.

AlSagheer, A. (2011). Six Sigma for sustainability in multinational organizations. *Journal of Business Case Studies, 7*, 7–15. Retrieved from http://www.journals.cluteonline.com

Anderson, J. C., Rungtusanatham, M., & Schroeder, R. G. (1994). A theory of quality management underlying the Deming management method. *Academy of Management. The Academy of Management Review, 19*, 472-509. doi:10.1111/j.1540-5915.1995.tb01444.x

Bacha, E. (2010). The relationships among organizational performance, environmental uncertainty, and employees' perceptions of CEO charisma. *The Journal of Management Development, 29*(1), 28-37. doi:10.1108/02621711011009054

Chu-Hua, K., Madu, C. N., & Chinho, L. (2008). Implementing supply chain quality management. *Total Quality Management & Business Excellence, 19*, 1127-1141. doi:10.1080/14783360802323511

Connell, M., & Fisher-Blando, J. (2013). Social responsibility of doctoral scholars. In C Lentz (Ed.), *Refractive thinker: Vol II: Effective research method & design for doctoral scholars*: (Chapter 8, pp. 153-170). Las Vegas, NV: The Refractive Thinker© Press.

Davila, T., Epstein, M. J., & Shelton, R. (2006). *Making innovation work: How to manage it, measure it, and profit from it* . Upper Saddle River, NJ: Pearson Education.

Dean, J. W., & Bowen, D. E. (1994). Management theory and total quality: Improving research and practice through theory development. *Academy of Management. The Academy of Management Review, 19*, 392-418. doi:10.1007/s10551-011-0833-x

Deming, W. E. (1986). *Out of the crisis.* Cambridge, MA: Massachusetts Institute of Technology.

Dragicevic, S., Celar, S., & Novak, L. (2011). Roadmap for requirements engineering process improvement using BMPN and UML. *Advances in Production Engineering & Management, 6*(3), 221-231. Retrieved from http://

apem-journal.org/

Fleming-Farrell, L. (2013). *A quantitative study of improvement program introduction frequency on organizational performance*. DBA dissertation, University of Phoenix, Arizona.

Florida Power & Light [FP&L]. (n.d.). *Quality awards and recognition*. Retrieved from http://www.fpl.com/about/quality/quality_awards_and_recognition.shtml

Florida Power & Light [FP&L]. (2013, November 14). *In Wikipedia, The Free Encyclopedia*. Retrieved from: http://en.wikipedia.org/w/index.php?title=Florida_Power_%26_Light&oldid=581665111

Foster, S. T. (2007). Does Six Sigma improve performance? *The Quality Management Journal, 14*(4), 7-20. Retrieved from http://www.ijser.org

George, J., & Jones, G. (2011*). Understanding and managing organizational behavior*. Upper Saddle River, NJ: Prentice-Hall.

Hall, E., & Knab, E.F. (2012, July). Social irresponsibility provides opportunity for the win-win-win of Sustainable Leadership. In C. A. Lentz (Ed.), *The refractive thinker: Vol. 7. Social responsibility* (pp. 197-220). Las Vegas, NV: The Refractive Thinker© Press.

Hall, E. B., & Hinkelman, R. M. (2013). *Perpetual Innovation™: A guide to strategic planning, patent commercialization and enduring competitive advantage*, Version 2.0. Morrisville, NC: LuLu Press.

Hames, R. D. (2007). The five literacies of global leadership: What authentic leaders know and you need to find out. San Francisco, CA: Jossey-Bass.

International Standards Organization [ISO]. (n.d.). ISO 9000– Management practices. Retrieved from http://www.iso.org/iso/iso_9000

Jones, G. R. (2010). *Organizational theory, design, and change* (6th ed.). Upper Saddle River, NJ: Prentice Hall.

Juran, M. J., & Gofrey, A. B. (1998). *Juran's quality handbook* (5th ed.). New York, NY: McGraw-Hill.

Kulach, P. S. (2013) *A quantitative correlational analysis between Six Sigma training and compensation of Six Sigma practitioners* (Doctoral dissertation). Retrieved from ProQuest (UMI No. 1449374282)

Leban, B., & Stone, R. (2008). *Managing organizational change*. New

York, NY: John Wiley & Sons.

Maurer, R. (2009). What's happening these days with change? *The Journal for Quality and Participation, 32*(2), 37-38. Retrieved from http://asq.org/pub/jqp/

Maurer, R. (2011). Why do so many changes still fail? (Part Two). *The Journal for Quality and Participation, 33*(4), 33-34. Retrieved fromhttp://asq.org/pub/jqp/

Maslow, A H. (1954). *Motivation and personality.* New York, NY: Harper and Row.

Mayo, E. (1949). *Hawthorne and the Western Electric Company: The social problems of an industrial civilisation.* Boston, MA: Routledge.

McShane, S., & Von Glinow, M. (2013). *Organizational behavior: Emerging knowledge and practice for the real world.* New York, NY: McGraw-Hill.

Mehra, S., Hoffman, J. M., & Sirias, D. (2001). TQM as a management strategy for the next millennia. *International Journal of Operations & Production Management, 21,* 855-876. doi:10.1108/02656710810908070

Pohl, K. (2010). *Requirements engineering: Fundamentals, principles, and techniques.* New York, NY: Springer.

Robbins, S. P., & Judge, T. A. (2011). *Organizational behavior* (14th ed.). Upper Saddle River, NJ: Pearson/Prentice Hall.

Rungtusanatham, M. (2008). From mass production to mass customization: Hindrance factors, structural inertia, and transition hazard. *Productions and Operations Management, 33.* doi:10.1007%2Fs11590-011-0303-5

Schermerhorn, J., Uhl-Bien, M., Hunt, J., & Osborn, R. (2011). *Organizational behavior.* Hoboken, NJ: Wiley.

Scott, W. R. (2003). *Organizations: Rational, natural, and open systems* (5th ed.). Upper Saddle River, NJ: Prentice Hall.

Scott, W. R., & Davis, G. F. (2007). *Organizations and organizing: Rational, natural, and open systems perspectives.* Upper Saddle River, NJ: Prentice Hall.

Seth, D., & Gupta, V. (2005). Application of value stream mapping for lean operations in cycle time reduction: an Indian case study. *Production &*

Planning Control, 16, 5. doi:10.1002/jso.2930160302

Six Sigma. (2014, February 13). In *Wikipedia, The Free Encyclopedia.* Retrieved from http://en.wikipedia.org/w/index.php?title=Six_Sigma&oldid=595273155

Walker, D., & Sorkin, S. (2007). *A-ha! Performance: Building and managing a self-motivated workforce.* New York, NY: John Wiley & Sons Inc.

Wehnert, U. (2009). *Implementing TQM cross-culturally: A mediated model of national culture dimensions, TQM values and organizational performance* (Doctoral dissertation). Retrieved from ProQuest. (UMI No. 3361225)

Weymann, E. (2001). Why change programs fail? *ASQ World Conference on Quality and Improvement Proceedings,* 582-585. Retrieved from http://asq.org/

Wheelen, T. L., & Hunger, J. Dl, (2012). *Concepts in strategic management and business policy: Toward global sustainability* (13th ed.). Upper Saddle River, NJ: Prentice-Hall.

Weick, K. E. (1969). *The social psychology of organizing.* Reading, MA: Addison-Wesley.

Weymann, E. (2001). Why change programs fail? *ASQ World Conference on Quality and Improvement Proceedings,* 582-585. Retrieved from http://asq.org/

Wiesendanger, B. (1993, September/October). Deming's luster dims at Florida Power & Light. *The Journal of Business Strategy, 14*(5), 60. doi:10.1108/eb039590

Yukl, G. (2010). Influencing organizational culture. In G. R. Hickman (Ed.), *Leading organizations: Perspectives for a new era* (2nd Ed.), (pp. 326-330). Thousand Oaks, CA: Sage.

Yukl, G. A. (2013). *Leadership in organizations* (8th ed.). Upper Saddle River, NJ: Pearson/Prentice Hall.

Zairi, M. (1994). Leadership in TQM implementation: Some case examples. *The TQM Magazine, 6*(6), 9-16. doi:10.1007/978-94-011-1302-1_10

About the Author...

Dr. Leo Fleming-Ferrell holds a Bachelor of Science (BSC Mgmt.) in Management Science from Trinity College Dublin, a Masters of Business Administration (MBA) Dublin City University and a Doctorate of Business Administration (DBA) from the University of Phoenix. He also holds a number of diplomas in industrial engineering, quality systems auditing. He has trained in the USA as a black belt in Six-Sigma.

Dr. Leo has more than 30 years, experience working in a wide range of manufacturing industries including, medical diagnostic chemicals, and precision laboratory liquid handling equipment, medical devices, printing, masterbatches, and plastics. He has held management positions both at national and international level in the areas of quality, operations, environment health and safety. Dr Leo has worked on five continents and lived in Germany, France, and Switzerland. He has returned to Ireland where he is *Head of Quality and Regulatory Affairs* for a medical device company.

Dr. Leo's main academic interests are in the practical application of continuous improvement and sustainability.

Dr. Leo Fleming-Farrell can be contacted at e-mail address leoflemingfarrell@hotmail.com

About the Author...

Dr. Elmer Hall *helps individuals and organizations plan for success that sustainably balances wellness and wealth.*

Dr. Elmer holds accredited degrees: BA and MBA from the University of South Florida; and Doctorate of International Business Administration (DIBA) from Nova Southeastern University. For 25 years, he taught business classes at several Florida universities, including Research Methods. He is a Facilitator and Dissertation Mentor for the University of Phoenix. His "real" education, however, is from his personal entrepreneurial ventures and those of clients.

Dr. Elmer is the President of Strategic Business Planning Company (www.SBPlan.com), doing strategic consulting for startups and expanding ventures. Major clients: IBM, Ryder, NextEra (FP&L), and Burger King (Diageo). He interned in *Quality Assurance*, NARF/NAS. At FP&L, he helped develop the quality improvement program (QIP) tools used throughout the company in the quest to win the *Deming Award.*

He publishes/consults on sustainability (in business and education), innovation, economic development, patent planning and Delphi/scenario planning. With Robert Hinkelman, he co-authored *Perpetual Innovation™: A Guide to Strategic Planning, Patent Commercialization and Enduring Competitive Advantage* and the *Patent Primer.* See http://www.lulu.com/spotlight/SBPlan/. Find SBP's Commercialization of Patent Assets (COMPASS®) process at www.IPplan.com

Blogs: http://www.SustainZine.com and http://ipzine.blogspot.com/

Twitter @ SBPlan and @PatentPlan

E-mail: Elmer@SBPlan.com

About the Author...

Southern California author Dr. Judy Fisher-Blando holds several accredited degrees: a Bachelor of Science (BS) in Business Management; a Master's of Art (MA) in Organizational Management; and a Doctorate of Management (DM) in Organizational Leadership from the University of Phoenix School of Advanced Studies. She has also obtained her Six Sigma Black Belt certificate.

Dr. Judy is an adjunct professor for Walden University, Capella University, and University of Phoenix, teaching classes in organizational behavior, ethical responsibility, and research methods. She is an expert on workplace bullying, writing her research dissertation about *Workplace Bullying: Aggressive Behavior and Its Effect on Job Satisfaction and Productivity.* In addition, she is a Life Coach, coaching leaders on how to develop High Performance Organizations, coaching the targets of workplace bullies, and giving presentations on Finding and Measuring your Joy.

To reach Dr. Judy Fisher-Blando for information on any of these topics, and for executive coaching or coaching for workplace bullying, please e-mail judyblando@gmail.com

CHAPTER 9

What Motivates Employees to Resign
and the Effects of Turnover

By Dr. David M. Mula and Dr. Eric L. Patterson

The cost of turnover is a highly debated subject with estimates that can range in excess of 150% of the lost employee's salary. Authors' of current literature acknowledge that turnover in organizations relates to high operational costs and decreased customer satisfaction (Hill & Bradley, 2010; Llorens & Stazyk, 2011). Turnover increases transactional costs and operational costs for organizations by increasing the manager to employee ratio, causing a loss of organizational knowledge that negatively affects customer satisfaction (Batt & Colvin, 2011; Carroll, Smith, & Oliver, 2008). The causes of turnover vary, but methods exist for mitigating turnover through better motivating and communicating with employees.

In this chapter, we will describe how understanding the motivations of employees to resign voluntarily can enable employers to leverage the power of communication and provide an opportunity to increase retention within their organization.

We will look at how encouraging the use of transformational leadership behaviors in leaders can enhance motivation and quality of work life for employees. Finally, we will examine the concept of emotional intelligence, and how it can enable employers to better understand employees and increase the chances of successfully using transformational leadership behaviors.

Understanding Employee Motivation

The loss of high-performers results in dysfunctional turnover within organizations (Patterson, 2013). Prior research focused on the relationship between employees and managers as the cause of dysfunctional turnover (Tremblay, Blanchard, Taylor, Pelletier, & Villeneuve, 2009). The ability to retain the best and brightest performers within organizations increases when talented employees are identified early and afforded development opportunities with competitive compensation. Understanding the lived experiences of customer service representatives provides insight into how employers can increase employee retention and increase productivity may reduce turnover costs related to recruiting, hiring, and training new employees (Cairncross & Kelly, 2008).

As employees become acclimated to the new responsibilities and processes of the job, at times, the actual tasks performed would seem different from the written job description versus the verbal communication about the job description. A psychological contract, an informal obligation between an employer and an employee, establishes when the employee conceives a specific expectation of the reward for his or her work (Cross, Barry, & Garavan, 2008; Hess & Jepsen, 2009). When employees encounter a lack of advancement opportunity, the psychological contract established between the employee and the employer is violated (Cross, Barry, & Garavan, 2008). Understanding how the psychological contract between employers and employees deteriorates underscores the importance of the factors that motivate employees.

The deterioration of the psychological contract between employers and employees increases the relevancy of the expectancy theory. Vroom (1964) describes that an employee's work effort is motivated by the expectation of receiving a specific reward for their work. Because the variation of employee emotions positively relates to effort, that in turn may affect the decision by employees to resign from organizations (Seo, Bartunek, & Feldman Barrett, 2010). Patterson (2013) identified eight primary themes as motivators for turnover, including (a) higher income opportunities, (b) phone-burnout, (c) limited career growth, (d) personal stress and anxiety, (e) alternative career options, (f) dissatisfaction with work environment, (g) frustration with corporate change, and (h) minimal management involvement as the primary motivators for resigning from the organization. While eight primary themes emerged from the Patterson study, the difference between the results when compared with other studies seemed to be linked to generational demographics. This finding provides insight to examine not only what causes turnover, but also who is most likely to resign in relation to specific motivators. For example, the most common recounted motivator to resign included a higher income opportunity. Of the 12 (60%) participants who identified the opportunity to earn more income as a motivator, 7 (58%) were female, a demographic that traditionally received lower wages (Moynihan & Pandey, 2008).

Findings from the participants in the Patterson (2013) study identified that 50% of the participants affirmed the initial decision to resign. Consequently, 25% of the participants indicated they would have made the decision to resign earlier, although the final 25% affirmed changing something about the decision to leave the company. This 25% of participants, and perhaps of employees in organizations, that could have their decisions to resign changed by how organizations manage knowledge about the contributing motivators to turnover. For example, participants in the Patterson study indicated that the participants strongly considered pursuing an alternate internal position, but decided to leave the company because of a lack of rapport with the current manager underling the importance of relationships between managers and employees (Doellgast, 2008; Holman et al., 2007).

Executives must closely examine employee demographics to understand and leverage the development from a work environment primarily comprised of Baby Boomers to an environment with a growing number of Generation X and Generation Y employees and how that transition affects turnover (Patterson, 2013). An examination of the generational demographics of employees in organizations can help to understand how the expectations of employees have changed since 2003. Prior research on turnover consistently associated the relationship of employees with their manager as the primary motivator of the decision to resign (Doellgast, 2008; Holman, Batt, & Holtgrewe, 2007). As more workers from Generation X and Generation Y enter the work force, the effect of generational perceptions upon the perception of work will have a larger greater role in turnover regarding the motivations to resign (Patterson, 2013). This change in generations changes the focus from why employees decide to resign from a monolithic approach to focusing on the motivations of specific segments (Patterson, 2013).

Younger employees from Generation X act interested in self-fulfillment, networking, and communicating in online communities that assist in establishing their career goals (Hess & Jepsen, 2009). Members of Generation X differ from Baby Boomers because members of Generation X grew up during a time of layoffs, or downsizing, and are not as trusting as Baby Boomers (Hess & Jepsen, 2009). Generation Y employees differ even further because Generation Y employees exhibit boredom and freely share their opinion of work conditions (Solnet & Hood, 2008). Employees who appeared uninterested to managers in organizations and did not receive support toward their career goals found a different company for which to work (Heijden, Schalk, & Veldhoven, 2008; Hess & Jepsen, 2009).

Patterson (2013) conducted a study in northeastern Kansas in which 50% of the participants were Generation Y employees. A modified van Kaam approach was used to analyze data collected from 20 participants in face-to-face and telephone interviews (Moustakas, 1994). Slaughter (2011) originally used the interview instrument in a qualitative study regarding why teachers in the state of Texas resigned their educational careers within the first 5 years of a teaching career. The instrument was used to examine the decisions by customer service representatives to resign. Semi-structured interviews posed 16 open-ended questions to customer service representatives that resigned voluntarily from their employer within the previous 5 years. The interview questions culminated in a final question posed to each participant; if you had to make the decision to leave the company again, what would you do differently? Each of the participants could reflect on the resignation decision and determine if given the opportunity, would he or she still choose to resign from the position.

The results of the Patterson (2013) study indicated that a working knowledge of changing generational motivations of turnover can be leveraged to reduce turnover related to pay, personal stress, and anxiety. Employee age had a significant effect upon turnover intentions as well. Generation X and Generation Y employees appeared less likely to remain with one employer (Hill & Bradley, 2008). The primary motivators associated with 20 call-center employees in northeastern Kansas were opportunities for higher income, phone burnout, and limited career growth. As Baby Boomers continue to transition to retirement age, employers will have to consider new ways to adjust retention strategies to include the contributing motivators of specific generations (Patterson, 2013).

Motivate More Effectively with Transformational Leadership

Transformational leadership behaviors can be a powerful tool in motivating employees through providing inspiration and purpose to their work. Transformational leaders rely on principles-based leadership behaviors that influence others to achieve organizational goals through change efforts and self-sacrifice (Gumusluoglu & Ilsev, 2009; Kendrick, 2011). This type of leader creates effects at multiple levels of organizational and social systems (Gumusluoglu & Ilsev, 2009; Kendrick, 2011). Transformational leadership consists of four dimensions, each of which researchers found plays a role in organizational and employee development. Idealized influence and inspirational motivation influence cohesion through visioning behaviors and involve rapport building, emphatic language, and commitment to the leader (Kouzes & Posner, 2011). Individualized consideration is a precursor to effective team communication and correlates with increased productivity and motivation (Kouzes & Posner, 2011). Leaders who encourage intellectual stimulation also encourage seeking different perspectives and viewing problems from multiple angles, which can promote functional and task-oriented conflict within the group (Kouzes & Posner, 2011).

Organizational leaders who embrace transformational leadership behaviors are less resistant to change and deal better with the rapidly evolving economy than leaders who do not display transformational leadership (Fitzgerald & Schutte, 2010; Oreg & Berson, 2011). A transformational leader shapes the organizational culture by actively managing talent and ensuring that individual passions, interests, and expertise help solve problems and improve processes (Bass, Avolio, Jung, & Berson, 2003; Carpenter, Fusfeld, & Gritzo, 2010; Polychroniou, 2009). The behaviors embraced by transformational leaders encourage the continual growth and evolution of leaders and employees by embracing new skillsets, and providing opportunities for both intellectual and professional growth (Eid, Johnsen, Bartone, & Nissestad, 2008). Workers are (a) more engaged, (b) achieve better outcomes, (c) innovate more effectively, and (d) possess higher levels of organizational commitment (Bushra, Usman, & Naveed, 2011; Fitzgerald & Schutte, 2010; Forest, & Kleiner, 2011; Marsh, 2010). The increased communication and empowerment typical of transformational environments reduce job stress and boost motivation creating an environment conducive to improved task performance and helping coworker behavior (Bono, Foldes, Vinson, & Muros, 2007; Farh, Seo, & Tesluk, 2012; Gill, Flaschner, & Bhutani, 2010; Tsai, Chen, & Cheng, 2009). Emphasis is placed on the collective interests of the team, inducing team members to place a high interest in membership and encouraging self-sacrifice for the good of the team (Eisenbeib & Boerner, 2010; Farh et al., 2012). A personal relationship of trust between the leader and employee allows the development of an intrinsic motivational attitude within the employee to achieve the leader's vision of the future (Herold, Fedor, Caldwell, & Liu, 2008).

Increased Understanding through Emotional Intelligence

Emotional intelligence evolved through continued studies, but a generally accepted model of emotional intelligence has four primary components (a) self-awareness, (b) self-management, (c) social awareness, and (d) relationship management (Wong & Law, 2002). Self-awareness and self-management are the abilities to know what emotion the individual is personally experiencing, why the individual is feeling that emotion, and how to control the emotion. Social awareness and relationship management both involve understanding the emotional environment the individual is operating in and building appropriate relationships within that environment.

A leader's effectiveness reading and interpreting employees', customers', and counterparts' emotional states during business relationships has multiple implications. Elizabeth and Wolff (2008) found that high levels of emotional intelligence in leaders positively influenced group norms and group performance. Leaders who understood their emotions made better decisions than those who repressed their emotions without trying to understand them first (Farh et al., 2012).

However, simply possessing a high level of emotional intelligence is not enough to be successful; the individual must be motivated to use these skills to achieve organizational goals (Rode et al., 2007). Emotional intelligence appears to act as an enabler of transformational leadership behaviors, enhancing the capability to harness and understand emotions making the use of transformational leadership behaviors even more effective. Researchers correlated high levels of emotional intelligence with a propensity to use transformational leadership behaviors (Awadzi Calloway, 2010; Farh et al., 2012; Hess & Bacigalupo, 2011; Mula, 2013; Tessema, 2010). Understanding the relationship between emotional intelligence and transformational leadership has been proven in other populations to create an environment to better train and develop leaders, overcome the after-effects of toxic leaders, and effect social change through improved employee morale, lowered levels of stress, increased productivity, and an increased ability as an agent of change (Polychroniou, 2009; Toor & Ofori, 2009).

Mula (2013) conducted a correlational and descriptive study to examine what relationships existed between emotional intelligence and transformational leadership in U.S. Army National Guard leaders (U.S. ARNG) leaders. The population consisted of leaders serving in the U.S. ARNG within a single state within the eastern United States. The organization chosen as the population was a brigade-size element consisting of approximately 2,171 soldiers and provided a population of approximately 989 leaders in the pay grades of E-5 through O-6. The researcher selected the organization for its varied composition of units representing the combat and combat service support functions of the U.S. Army. The Wong and Law Emotional Intelligence Scale (WLEIS) measured emotional intelligence scores along four dimensions: (a) self-emotion appraisal, (b) others emotional appraisal, (c) regulation of emotion, and (d) use of emotions. The Leadership Practices Inventory (LPI) measured transformational leadership behaviors along the dimensions of (a) model the way, (b) inspire a shared vision, (c) challenge the process, (d) enable others to act, and (e) encourage the heart (Kouzes & Posner, 2011). Both the WLEIS and the LPI are established instruments tested for reliability and validity (Posner, 2010; Wong & Law, 2002). Statistical Package for the Social Sciences (SPSS) version 21.0 was used for the data analyses. Results indicated significant relationships were found between emotional intelligence and transformational leadership, as well as between age and emotional intelligence. Mula found a strong positive relationship between emotional intelligence and transformational leadership, r (101) = .671, p < .001, and weak negative relationship between age and emotional intelligence, r(101) = -.289, p = .003 (Mula, 2013). These findings supported previous researchers' findings that emotional intelligence and transformational leadership positively relate and added to the body of literature that emotional intelligence correlated with age (Awadzi Calloway, 2010; Martini, 2008; Meredith, 2007; Tessema, 2010).

Findings in the Mula (2013) study indicated an opportunity to affect organizational change through developing training programs to improve emotional intelligence and transformational leadership in U.S. ARNG leaders. Perhaps most importantly, the results align with previous researchers' findings in the fields of emotional intelligence and transformational leadership within other similar populations, which indicate relationships exist across populations and are not limited strictly to the military (Awadzi Calloway, 2010; Martini, 2008; Meredith, 2007; Mula, 2013; Tessema, 2010). Implementing these findings could provide direct, tangible improvements to both leaders and those they lead.

Transformational leaders often work beyond minimum requirements highlighting the importance of diversity management, placing an emphasis on ensuring fair treatment and protecting the welfare of individuals, which result in greater levels of corporate social responsibility (Kendrick, 2011; Ng & Sears, 2012). Employees with supervisors who rated high on emotional intelligence scales experienced more positive emotions throughout their day, and those with supervisors who rate low on emotional intelligence scales, experienced greater levels of stress in the workplace (Bono et al., 2007). The increased use of transformational leadership behaviors leads to improved employee morale, productivity, and success acting as a change agent within organizations (Polychroniou, 2009; Toor & Ofori, 2009).

Conclusion

Turnover costs can be incredibly expensive in both financial and non-financial ways. Replacing employees who choose to leave adds additional expenses to the corporate bottom line, reduces employee motivation, and hurts customer satisfaction. Communicating with employees is key to ensuring strategic alignment within the organization. It is imperative that every employee understands how their contribution to the organization achieves the overall goals and vision of the company. When employees understand the value of their work, they develop an attitude of intrinsic motivation to achieve their goals and the company goals. Understanding how to communicate with and motivate employees is necessary to reducing turnover, especially with the current mix of generations in the workforce.

Expectancy theory helps leaders understand turnover better because an employee's effort and motivation relates to the manifestation of rewards and payment for his or her work effort (Vroom, 1964). Employee effort, orientation, and persistence directly relate to active immediate feelings (Seo, Bartunek, & Feldman Barrett, 2010). Understanding that the goals and expectations of employees affect behavioral performance and motivation allows employers to intervene and create an environment conducive to positive orientation (Seo & Ilies, 2009). Transformational leadership behaviors are another method available to increase motivation in employees. These behaviors increase motivation, organizational commitment, and improve employee morale, which positively influence turnover. Providing greater levels of inspiration and purpose to the workforce aligns with the expectations of the Generation X and Y workforce currently moving into leadership positions. Finally, emotional intelligence has been shown to positively correlate with the use of transformational leadership behaviors and enhance the harnessing and understanding of emotions. Leaders with high levels of emotional intelligence are expected to better determine employee motivation and show a greater use of transformational leadership behaviors, both of which may result in decreased turnover costs.

Thoughts from the Academic Entrepreneur™

The problem to be solved:
- The high cost of employee turnover

The goals:
- To find effective methods for mitigating turnover through better motivating and communicating with employees.

The questions to ask:
- How can the concept of emotional intelligence enable employers to better understand employees and increase the chances of successfully using transformational leadership behaviors?

Today's Business Application:

- Employee turnover is rarely caused by violation of the written contract between employee and employer, but rather the unspoken social contract that arises after a certain period on the job.
- Employees from Generation X differ from the Baby Boomers in their unwritten expectations, are generally less trusting and expect more opportunities to build their personal careers. Employees from Generation Y differ from the Baby Boomers even more so.
- Having high Emotional Intelligence alone is not enough to retain employees. Managerial habits related to High Emotional Intelligence will help lower employee turnover.

References

Awadzi Calloway, J. D. (2010). *Performance implications of emotional intelligence and transformational leadership: Toward the development of a self-efficacious military leader* (Doctoral dissertation). Available from ProQuest Dissertations and Theses database. (UMI No. 3413132)

Bass, B. M., Avolio, B. J., Jung, D. I., & Berson, Y. (2003). Predicting unit performance by assessing transformational and transactional leadership. *Journal of Applied Psychology, 88*, 207-218. doi:10.1037/0021-9010.88.2.207

Batt, R., & Colvin, A. (2011). An employment systems approach to turnover: human resources practices, quits, dismissals, and performance. *Academy of Management Journal, 54*, 695-717. doi:10.5465/AMJ.2011.64869448

Bono, J. E., Foldes, H. J., Vinson, G., & Muros, J. P. (2007). Workplace emotions: The role of supervision and leadership. *Journal of Applied Psychology, 92*, 1357-1367. doi:10.1037/0021-9010.92.5.1357

Bushra, F., Usman, A., & Naveed, A. (2011). Effect of transformational leadership on employees' job satisfaction and organizational commitment in banking sector of Lahore. *International Journal of Business and Social Science, 2*, 261-267. Retrieved from http://www.ijbssnet.com/update/

Cairncross, G., & Kelly, S. (2008). Human resource development and 'casualisation' in hotels and resorts in eastern Australia: Getting the best to the customer? *Journal of Management & Organization, 14*, 367-385. doi:10.5172/jmo.837.14.4.367

Carpenter, D. J., Fusfeld, A. R., & Gritzo, L. A. (2010). Leadership skills and styles. *Research Technology Management, 53*(6), 58-60. Retrieved from http://www.iriweb.org/

Carroll, M., Smith, M., & Oliver, G. (2008). Recruitment and retention in front-line services: The case of childcare. *Human Resource Management Journal, 19*, 59-74. doi:10.1111/j.1748-8583.2008.00076.x

Cassidy, D., & Sutherland, J. (2008). Going absent, then just going? A case study examination of absence and quitting. *Economic Issues, 13*, 1-19.

Retrieved from http://www.economicissues.org.uk/

Cross, C., Barry, G., & Garavan, T. P. (2008). The psychological contract in call centres: An employee perspective. *Journal of Industrial Relations, 50,* 229-242. doi:10.1177/0022185607087899

Dalton, D. R., Krackhardt, D. M., & Porter, L. W. (1981). Functional turnover: An empirical assessment. Journal of Applied Psychology, *66,* 716-721. doi:10.1037/00219010.66.6.716dissertation). Available from ProQuest Dissertations and Theses database. (UMI No. 3588132)

Doellgast, V. (2008). Collective bargaining and high involvement management in comparative perspective: Evidence from U.S and German call centers. *Industrial Relations, 47,* 284-319. doi:10.111/j.1468-232x.2008.00521.x

Eid, J., Johnsen, B. H., Bartone, P. T., & Nissestad, O. A. (2008). Growing transformational leaders: Exploring the role of personality hardiness. *Leadership & Organization Development Journal, 29,* 4-23. doi:10.1108/01437730810845270

Eisenbeib, S., & Boerner, S. (2010). Transformational leadership and R&D innovation: Taking a curvilinear approach. *Creativity & Innovation Management, 19,* 364-372. doi:10.1111/j.1467-8691.2010.00563.x

Elizabeth, S. K., & Wolff, S. B. (2008). Emotional intelligence competencies in the team and team leader. *The Journal of Management Development, 27,* 55-75. doi:10.1108/02621710810840767

Farh, C., Seo, M., & Tesluk, P. E. (2012). Emotional intelligence, teamwork effectiveness, and job performance: The moderating role of job context. *Journal of Applied Psychology, 97,* 890-900. doi:10.1037/a0027377

Fitzgerald, S., & Schutte, N. S. (2010). Increasing transformational leadership through enhancing self-efficacy. *Journal of Management Development, 29,* 495-505. doi:10.1108/02621711011039240

Forest, M., & Kleiner, B. (2011). Effects of current nursing management styles on the retention and recruitment of nurses: A review of the literature. *International Journal of Management Reviews, 28,* 254-262. Retrieved from http://www.internationaljournalofmanagement.co.uk/

Gill, A., Flaschner, A., & Bhutani, S. (2010). The impact of transformational leadership and empowerment on employee job stress. *Business and Economics Journal, 2010*(BEJ-3), 1-11. Retrieved from http://astonjournals.com/bej

Gumusluoglu, L., & Ilsev, A. (2009). Transformational leadership, creativity, and organizational innovation. *Journal of Business Research, 62*, 461-473. doi:10.1016/j.jbusres.2007.07.032

Heijden, B. I. J. M. V. D., Schalk, R., & Veldhoven, M. J. P. M. V. (2008). Aging and Careers: European research on long-term career development and early retirement. *Career Development International, 13*, 85-94. doi:10.1108/13620430810860512

Herold, D. M., Fedor, D. B., Caldwell, S., & Liu, Y. (2008). The effects of transformational and change leadership on employees' commitment to a change: A multilevel study. *Journal of Applied Psychology, 93*, 346-357. doi:10.1037/0021-9010.93.2.346

Hess, J. D., & Bacigalupo, A. C. (2011). Enhancing decisions and decision-making processes through the application of emotional intelligence skills. *Management Decision, 49*, 710-721. doi:10.1108/00251741111130805

Hess, N., & Jepsen, D. M. (2009). Career stage and generational differences in psychological contracts. *Career Development International, 14*, 261-283. doi:10.1108/13620430910966433

Hill, T., & Bradley, C. (2010). The emotional consequences of service work: An ethnographic examination of hair salon workers. *Sociological Focus, 43*, 41-60. Retrieved from http://www.sociologicalfocus.net/

Holman, D., Batt, R., & Holtgrewe, U. (2007). The global call center report: International perspectives on management and employment. *Report of the Global Call Center Network*. Retrieved from http://www.globalcallcenter.org

Kendrick, J. (2011). Transformational leadership changing individuals & social systems. *Professional Safety, 56*(11), 14-15. Retrieved from http://www.asse.org

Kouzes, J. M., & Posner, B. Z. (2011). *The five practices of exemplary leadership* (2nd ed.). San Francisco, CA: Pfeiffer.

Llorens, J., & Stazyk, E. (2011). How important are competitive wages? Exploring the impact of relative wage rates on employee turnover in state government. *Review of Public Personnel Administration, 31*, 111-127. doi:10.1177/0734371x10386184

Marsh, F. K. (2010). High performance team: Building a business program with part- and full-time faculty. *Journal of Education for Business, 85*, 187-194. doi:10.1080/08832320903252421

Martini, P. (2008). *Toward an integrated model of visionary leadership: A multilevel study* (Doctoral dissertation). Available from ProQuest Dissertations and Theses database. (UMI No. 3340923)

Meredith, C. (2007). *The relationship of emotional intelligence and transformational leadership behavior in non-profit executive leaders* (Doctoral dissertation). Retrieved from Dissertation Abstracts International. (UMI No. 3290654)

Moustakas, C. E. (1994). *Phenomenological research methods.* Thousand Oaks, CA: Sage.

Moynihan, D. P., & Pandey, S. K. (2008). The ties that bind: Social networks, person-organization value fit, and turnover intention. *Journal of Public Administration Research and Theory, 18*, 205-227. doi:10.1093/jopart/mum013

Mula, D. M. (2013). *Examining emotional intelligence and transformational leadership within U.S. Army National Guard leaders* (Doctoral dissertation). Available from ProQuest Dissertations and Theses database. (UMI No. 3566508)

Ng, E., & Sears, G. (2012). CEO leadership styles and the implementation of organizational diversity practices: Moderating effects of social values and age. *Journal of Business Ethics, 105*, 41-52. doi:10.1007/s10551-011-0933-7

Oreg, S., & Berson, Y. (2011). Leadership and employees' reactions to change: The role of leaders' personal attributes and transformational leadership style. *Personnel Psychology, 64*, 627-659. doi:10.1111/j.1744-6570.2011.01221.x

Patterson, E. L. (2013). *An exploratory study on call-center turnover in Northeastern Kansas* (Doctoral dissertation). Available from ProQuest

Dissertations and Theses database. (UMI No. 3588132)

Piercy, N., & Rich, N. (2009). High quality and low cost: The lean service centre. *European Journal of Marketing, 43*, 1477-1497. doi:10.1108/03090560910989993

Polychroniou, P. V. (2009). Relationship between emotional intelligence and transformational leadership of supervisors. *Team Performance Management, 15*, 343-356. doi:10.1108/13527590911002122

Posner, B. Z. (2010). *Leadership practices inventory (LPI) data analysis.* Santa Clara, CA: Santa Clara University.

Rode, J. C., Mooney, C. H., Arthaud-Day, M. L., Near, J. P., Baldwin, T. T., Rubin, R. S., & Bommer, W. H. (2007). Emotional intelligence and individual performance: Evidence of direct and moderated effects. *Journal of Organizational Behavior, 28*, 399-421. doi:10.1002/job.429

Seo, M., & Ilies, R. (2009). The role of self-efficacy, goal, and affect in dynamic motivational self-regulation. *Organizational Behavior and Human Decision Processes, 109*, 120-133. doi.org/10.1016/j.obhdp.2009.03.001

Seo, M., Bartunek, J. M., & Feldman Barrett, L. (2010). The role of affective experience in work motivation: Test of a conceptual model. *Journal of Organizational Behavior, 31*, 951-968. doi:10.1002/job655

Slaughter, J. (2011). *A phenomenological examination of early attrition among early career teachers* (Doctoral dissertation). Available from ProQuest Dissertations and Theses database. (UMI No. 3481028)

Solnet, D., & Hood, A. (2008). Generation Y as hospitality employees: Framing a research agenda. *Journal of Hospitality and Tourism Management, 15*, 59-68. doi:10.1375/jhtm.15.4.59

Tessema, D. B. (2010). *The relationship between emotional intelligence and transformational leadership in project management: A quantitative study* (Doctoral dissertation). Available from ProQuest Dissertations and Theses database. (UMI No. 3402253)

Toor, S., & Ofori, G. (2009). Ethical leadership: Examining the relationships with full range leadership model, employee outcomes, and organizational culture. *Journal of Business Ethics, 90*, 533-547. doi:10.1007/s10551-009-0059-3

Tremblay, M., Blanchard, C., Taylor, S., Pelletier, L., & Villeneuve, M. (2009). Work extrinsic and intrinsic motivation scale: Its value for organizational psychology research. *Canadian Journal of Behavioral Science, 41*, 213-226. doi:10.1037/a0015167

Tsai, W., Chen, H., & Cheng, J. (2009). Employee positive moods as a mediator linking transformational leadership and employee work outcomes. *The International Journal of Human Resource Management, 20*, 206-219. doi:10.1080/09585190802528714

Visser, W. A., & Rothmann, S. (2009). The development of a hassle-based diagnostic scale for predicting burnout in call centres. *South African Journal of Human Resource Management, 7*, 92-99. doi:10.4102/sai/hrm.v7i1.181

Vroom, V. (1964). *Work and motivation*. New York NY: John Wiley & Sons.

Wong, C. S., & Law, K. S. (2002). The effects of leader and follower emotional intelligence on performance and attitude: An exploratory study. *The Leadership Quarterly, 13*, 243-274. doi:10.1016/s1048-9843(02)00099-1

About the Author...

Dr. David M. Mula resides in New Orleans, Louisiana. Dr. Mula holds several accredited degrees; a Bachelor of Science (BS) in Business from Upper Iowa University; a Master of Business Administration (MBA) from Upper Iowa University; and a Doctorate of Business Administration (DBA) from Walden University.

Dr. David is a Faculty Member at University of Phoenix and Upper Iowa University, approved to teach business, management, organizational behavior, ethics, and leadership at the undergraduate and graduate level. He is a member of Psi Chi, Phi Beta Lambda, and the Enlisted Association of the National Guard of the United States.

Dr. David is a Master Sergeant in the Louisiana Army National Guard, trained as an intelligence analyst, and has served since 1995. He is currently the Operations NCO for the 139th Regional Support Group. Dr. David also serves as the co-chair of the Army Communities of Excellence Committee, responsible for annually assessing the business practices of the Louisiana Army National Guard using the Baldrige Criteria for Performance Excellence. His doctoral study, *Examining Emotional Intelligence and Transformational Leadership within U.S. Army National Guard Leaders*, provided him the opportunity to gain professional and academic expertise to recommend improvements in the training of military personnel.

To reach Dr. David M. Mula for information on consulting or doctoral coaching, please e-mail: david.mula@me.com

About the Author...

Dr. Eric L. Patterson lives in Topeka, Kansas. Dr. Eric holds multiple degrees; a Bachelor of Science (BS) from Baker University; a Master of Business Administration (MBA) from Friends University; and a Doctorate of Business Administration (DBA) with an emphasis on Leadership from Walden University.

Dr. Eric is an Adjunct Faculty Member at Rasmussen College approved to teach business management courses and has worked as a manager in the automotive finance, insurance, and call-center industries for 14 years. He also serves on two corporate boards; Treasurer of Child Care Aware of Eastern Kansas, Inc. and board member of the Ronald McDonald House Charities of Topeka, KS. His doctoral study, *An Exploratory Study on Call-Center Turnover in Northeastern Kansas*, provided him the opportunity to gain professional and academic expertise to recommend improvements in the retention of call-center employees.

To reach Dr. Eric L. Patterson for information of consulting or doctoral coaching, please email: epericsr@gmail.com

Epilogue

The Refractive Thinker®: Business Results From
Academic Research

By Dr. Cheryl Lentz and Ron Klein

Thank you for joining us through our journey to learn more about these fascinating areas if academic research regarding management, communication, and motivation. While the scholars of this 10th volume of The Refractive Thinker® offered their research findings and insights better than we ever could, let us conclude our journey by pondering the following question:

What can we take away from this research beyond the ideas of nine very smart teams of people?

"Plenty!" we would say. A bigger idea at work here is one that deserves a few moments of our time together to reflect on its deeper meaning.

There is more here than just the ideas nurtured in this journal being interesting or well thought-out. These teams' findings are more than just decorative set pieces designed to secure academic credentials. Instead, these chapters offer systems of ideas that **can save your business significant sums of money**, explained in ways that lend themselves to application. The implementation of each idea may be wrapped in the language of the academic scholar, but any business owner knows there is potential gold within academic research. Our purpose is to find this connection to translate and transfer research results from academia into the hands of the business owner.

Business people and other practically minded individuals often struggle with the world of abstract thought and pure knowledge, where this edition of *The Refractive Thinker®* proves beyond a doubt that their attitude requires the ability to translate pearls of research wisdom into practical business application. Abstract, academic thought can (and often does) produce concrete, actionable pieces of information that business owners like us can then take to the bank. The bigger lesson and take away here is that if you are a business owner, let's not immediately discount an idea just because it comes from those within academic circles. Remember, Dr. Albert Einstein changed the worlds of academia and business with his wonderful ideas that first began with theoretical thinking and abstract reflection within the hallowed halls of academia. This result is the first half of our point.

The world of academia can learn more than a few things from the world of business as well. Yes, academics often produce valuable ideas . . . but often these ideas may be buried behind abstract language, unique formats, and within exclusive academic communities. Each industry speaks its own language, where an accountant speaks differently than an engineer, where academicians are no different. If there is one thing that business people understand, it is that presentation is important! One can have the most amazing product in the world, yet it won't matter a bit if these ideas miss connecting to potential customers.

This ability to connect to one's audience is truer than ever within the areas of business with the continuing maturity of the Internet. Knowledge and information that are old or outdated have fallen away or become irrelevant. Information in this past faced society needs to be current and timely, as well as relevant to the needs of business. If academia wishes to maintain (or even increase) its level of relevancy in the modern world, academics will eventually have to address the question of presentation. How can one connect the world of theory and research into the practical needs of the business world? Herein lies where academics can learn from the masters of the business world.

As we end this volume, the bigger lessons for us to consider are how to get research out of the hallowed halls of academia, off the coffee table so to speak, and into the hands of those in the business world who can change lives with these research results and potential benefits. We need to bridge this gap between these two worlds to build bridges where academics and business owners can travel freely in both directions. After all, the goal is to affect and influence the world in which we live. The reality is that research can change people's lives, particularly when placed in the hands of business owners who can implement what academics have discovered. What wonderful synergy when this relationship works!

In the end, it's all about being open to communication—just like these scholars have been saying for the past 100 pages!

Wishing you every success!

INDEX

The Refractive Thinker®

AND

Pensiero Press

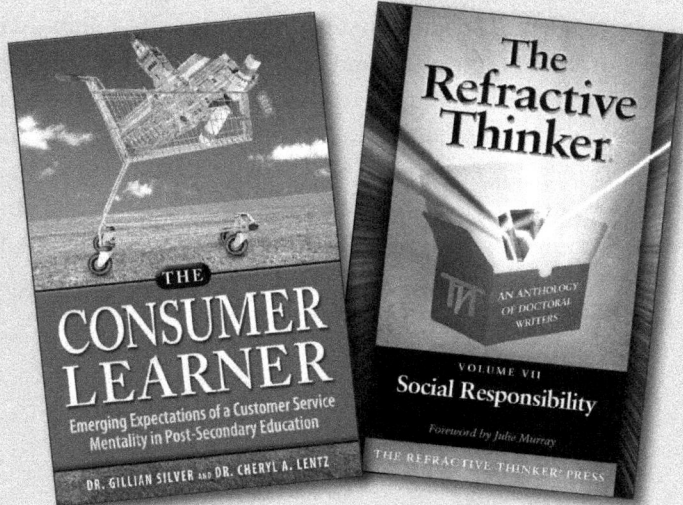

THE
CONSUMER LEARNER
Emerging Expectations of a Customer Service
Mentality in Post-Secondary Education
DR. GILLIAN SILVER and DR. CHERYL A. LENTZ

The
Refractive Thinker
AN ANTHOLOGY
OF DOCTORAL
WRITERS
VOLUME VII
Social Responsibility
Foreword by Julie Murray
THE REFRACTIVE THINKER® PRESS

2014 CATALOG

The Refractive Thinker®:
An Anthology of Higher Learning

The Refractive Thinker® Press
7124 Glyndon Trail NW
Albuquerque, NM 87114 USA

info@refractivethinker.com
www.refractivethinker.com
blog: www.dissertationpublishing.com

Books are available through The Refractive Thinker® Press at special discounts for bulk purchases for the purpose of sales promotion, seminar attendance, or educational purposes. Special volumes can be created for specific purposes and to organizational specifications. Orders placed on www.refractivethinker.com for students and military receive a 15% discount. Please contact us for further details.

Refractive Thinker® logo by Joey Root; The Refractive Thinker® Press logo design by Jacqueline Teng, cover design by Peri Poloni-Gabriel, Knockout Design (www.knockoutbooks.com), production by Gary A. Rosenberg (www.thebookcouple.com).

Pensiero Press

Pensiero Press
7124 Glyndon Trail NW
Albuquerque, NM 87114 USA

I *think* therefore I am.

—RENEE DESCARTES

I *critically think* to be.
I *refractively think* to change the world.

THANK YOU FOR JOINING US as we continue to celebrate the accomplishments of doctoral scholars affiliated with many phenomenal institutions of higher learning. The purpose of the anthology series is to share a glimpse into the scholarly works of participating authors on various subjects.

The Refractive Thinker® serves the tenets of leadership, which is not simply a concept outside of the self, but comes from within, defining our very essence; where the search to define leadership becomes our personal journey, not yet a finite destination.

The Refractive Thinker® is an intimate expression of who we are: the ability to think beyond the traditional boundaries of thinking and critical thinking. Instead of mere reflection and evaluation, one challenges the very boundaries of the constructs itself. If thinking is *inside* the box, and critical thinking is *outside* the box, we add the next step of refractive thinking, *beyond* the box. Perhaps the need exists to dissolve the box completely. As in our first four volumes, the authors within these pages are on a mission to change the world. They are never satisfied or quite content with *what is* or asking *why,* instead these authors intentionally strive to push and test the limits to ask *why not.*

We look forward to your interest in discussing future opportunities. Let our collection of authors continue the journey initiated with Volume I, to which *The Refractive Thinker*® will serve as our guide to future volumes. Come join us in our quest to be refractive thinkers and add your wisdom to the collective. We look forward to your stories.

Please contact The Refractive Thinker® Press for information regarding these authors and the works contained within these pages. Perhaps you or your organization may be looking for an author's expertise to incorporate as part of your annual corporate meetings as a keynote or guest speaker(s), perhaps to offer individual, or group seminars or coaching, or require their expertise as consultants.

Join us on our continuing adventures of *The Refractive Thinker*® where we expand the discussion specifically begun in Volume I with leadership; Volume II with Research Methodology (now in its 2nd Edition); Volume III with Change Management; Volume IV with Ethics, Leadership, and Globalization; Volume V with Strategy in Innovation, Volume VI with Post-Secondary Education, and Volume VII with Social Responsibility—all themed to explore the realm of strategic thought, creativity, and innovation.

Dr. Cheryl A. Lentz, managing editor of The Lentz Leadership Institute, explains the unique benefits of the books for readers:

"They celebrate the diffusion of innovative refractive thinking through the writings of these doctoral scholars as they dare to think differently in search of new applications and understandings of research methodology. Unlike most academic books that merely define research, The Refractive Thinker® *offers unique applications of research methodologies from the perspective of multiple authors—each offering a chapter based on their specific expertise."*

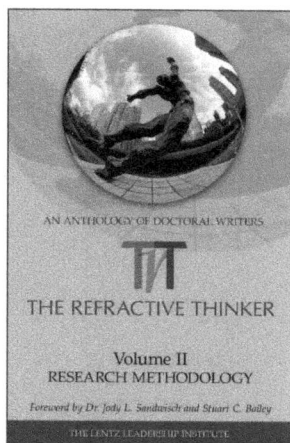

The Refractive Thinker®: Volume II: Research Methodology

The authors within these pages are on a mission to change the world, never satisfied or quite content with what is or asking *why,* instead these authors intentionally strive to push and test the limits to ask *why not. The Refractive Thinker®* is an intimate expression of who we are—the ability to think beyond the traditional boundaries of thinking and critical thinking. Instead of mere reflection and evaluation, one challenges the very boundaries of the constructs itself.

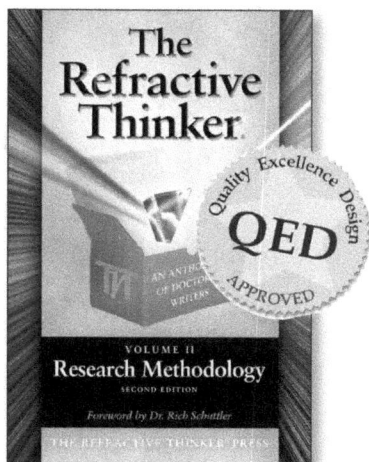

The Refractive Thinker®: Volume II: Research Methodology, 2nd Edition

**Chosen as Finalist, Education/Academic category
The USA "Best Books 2011" Awards,
sponsored by USA Book News**

As in Volume I, the authors within these pages are on a mission to change the world, never satisfied or quite content with what is or asking *why,* instead these authors intentionally strive to push and test the limits to ask *why not. The Refractive Thinker®* is an intimate expression of who we are—the ability to think beyond the traditional boundaries of thinking and critical thinking. Instead of mere reflection and evaluation, one challenges the very boundaries of the constructs itself.

For more information, please visit our website: www.refractivethinker.com

The Refractive Thinker®: Volume III: Change Management

This next offering in the series shares yet another glimpse into the scholarly works of these authors, specifically on the topic of change management. In addition to exploring various aspects of change management, the purpose of *The Refractive Thinker®* is also to serve the tenets of leadership. Leadership is not simply a concept outside of the self, but comes from within, defining our very essence; where the search to define leadership becomes our personal journey, not yet a finite destination.

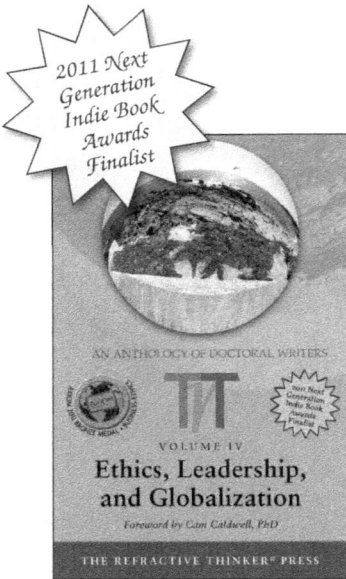

The Refractive Thinker®: Volume IV: Ethics, Leadership, and Globalization

The purpose of this volume is to highlight the scholarly works of these authors on the topics of ethics, leadership, and concerns within the global landscape of business. Join us as we venture forward to showcase the authors of Volume IV, and continue to celebrate the accomplishments of these doctoral scholars affiliated with many phenomenal institutions of higher learning.

For more information, please visit our website: www.refractivethinker.com

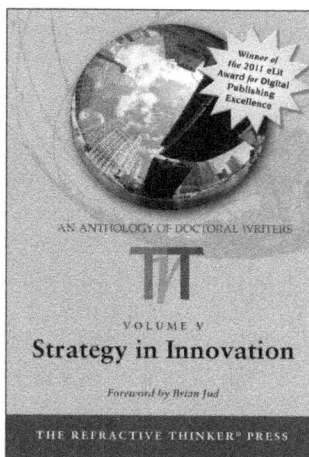

The Refractive Thinker Press Wins 2011 eLit Award for Digital Publishing Excellence

July 2, 2012, Las Vegas, NV—*The Refractive Thinker: Vol. V: Strategy in Innovation* has been named the winner of the Gold in the Anthology category of the 2011 eLit Awards!

The Refractive Thinker®: Volume VI: Post-Secondary Education

Celebrate the diffusion of innovative refractive thinking through the writings of these doctoral scholars as they dare to think differently in search of new applications and understandings of post-secondary education. Unlike most academic books that merely define research, *The Refractive Thinker®* offers commentary regarding the state of post-secondary education from the perspective of multiple authors—each offering a chapter based on their specific expertise.

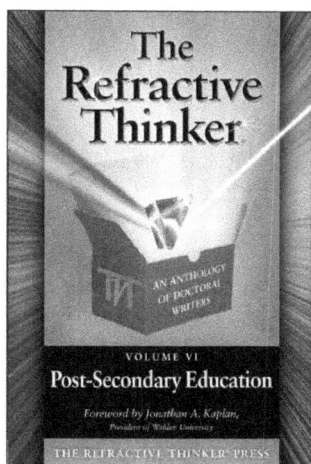

For more information, please visit our website: www.refractivethinker.com

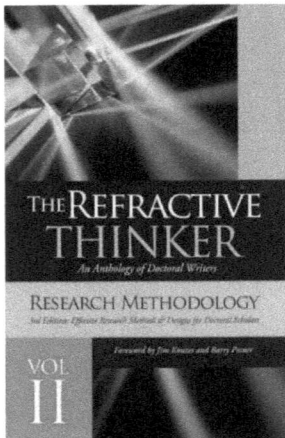

The Refractive Thinker® : Volume II: Research Methodology, 3rd Edition

If thinking is inside the box, and critical thinking is outside the box, refractive thinking is beyond the box. The Refractive Thinker® series provides doctoral scholars with a collaborative opportunity to promote and publish their work in a peer reviewed publication, which meets the university standard. Our goal is to provide an affordable outlet for scholars that supports the tremendous need for dynamic dialogue and innovation while providing an additional clout and recognition for each.

For more information, please visit our website: www.refractivethinker.com

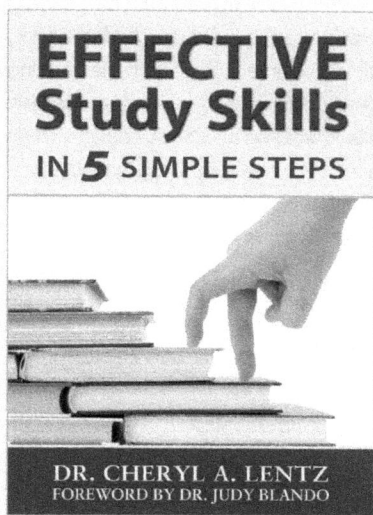

EFFECTIVE
Study Skills
IN **5** SIMPLE STEPS

Dr. Cheryl Lentz has compiled the valuable information she gives in her blog in one easy-to-use handbook. The study tips are designed to help any student improve learning and understanding, and ultimately earn higher grades. The handbook is not so large that it requires long hours of reading, as is the case with many books on the subject. The information is written in a manner to help a learner "see" and "practice" proven study techniques. Effective study skills must be practiced to for improvement to occur.

PUBLICATIONS ORDER FORM

Please send the following books:

- ❑ *The Refractive Thinker®* : Volume I: An Anthology of Higher Learning
- ❑ *The Refractive Thinker®* : Volume II: Research Methodology
- ❑ *The Refractive Thinker®* : Volume II: Research Methodology, 2nd Edition
- ❑ *The Refractive Thinker®* : Volume II: Research Methodology, 3rd Edition
- ❑ *The Refractive Thinker®* : Volume III: Change Management
- ❑ *The Refractive Thinker®* : Volume IV: Ethics, Leadership and Globalization
- ❑ *The Refractive Thinker®* : Volume V: Strategy in Innovation
- ❑ *The Refractive Thinker®* : Volume VI: Post-Secondary Education
- ❑ *The Refractive Thinker®* : Volume VII: Social Responsibility

Please contact the Refractive Thinker® Press for book prices, e-book prices, and shipping.
Individual e-chapters available by author: $3.95 (plus applicable tax). www.refractivethinker.com

---

- ❑ *The Consumer Learner: Emergence and Expectations of a Customer Service Mentality in Post-Secondary Education*
- ❑ *Effective Study Skills in 5 Simple Steps*
- ❑ *Journey Outside the Golden Palace*

Please send more FREE information:

❑ Speaking engagements ❑ Educational seminars ❑ Consulting

Join our Mailing List

Name: _____

Address:_____

City: _____ State:_____ Zip: _____

Telephone: _____ Email:_____

Sales tax: NV Residents please add 8.1% sales tax

Shipping: *Please see our website for shipping rates.*

Please mail or e-mail form to:

The Refractive Thinker® Press/
  Pensiero Press
7124 Glyndon Trail NW
Albuquerque, NM 87114 USA
E-mail: orders@lentzleadership.com
www.refractivethinker.com

Participation in
Future Volumes of
The Refractive Thinker®

Yes, I would like to participate in:

❏ **Doctoral Volume**(s) for a specific university or organization:

Name: _____

Contact Person: _____

Telephone: _____ E-mail: _____

❏ **Specialized Volume**(s) Business or Themed:

Name: _____

Contact Person: _____

Telephone: _____ E-mail: _____

Please mail or e-mail form to:

The Refractive Thinker® Press
7124 Glyndon Trail NW
Albuquerque, NM 87114 USA
E-mail: orders@lentzleadership.com
www.refractivethinker.com

Join us on Twitter, LinkedIn, and Facebook

www.ingramcontent.com/pod-product-compliance
Lightning Source LLC
Chambersburg PA
CBHW060406220326
41598CB00023B/3042